THE SHOC
YOU CAN'T PUT DOWN...

THE VITAL MESSAGE
YOU CAN'T IGNORE.

CULTS THAT KILL

Also by Larry Kahaner

ON THE LINE

CULTS THAT KILL

Probing the Underworld of Occult Crime

LARRY KAHANER

WARNER BOOKS

A Warner Communications Company

WARNER BOOKS EDITION

Illustrations: Howard Roberts
Cover design by Judith Leeds
Cover photograph by Simon Metz

Warner Books, Inc.
666 Fifth Avenue
New York, N.Y. 10103

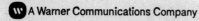 A Warner Communications Company

Printed in the United States of America

This book was originally published in hardcover by Warner Books.
First Printed in Paperback: November, 1989

10 9 8 7 6 5 4

TABLE OF CONTENTS

INTRODUCTION

This book began as an investigation into the growing phenomenon of Satanism in America. It was to be a study of Satanists, their beliefs and practices. As I interviewed more and more people living in this bizarre and mysterious world, however, what I found led me in a different direction. I found a hidden society, much larger and more disquieting than the world of Satanism alone, a place few people know exists.

It is the underworld of "occult crime," and it's the most-discussed issue in law enforcement circles today. The crimes are frightening: a homicide where the decapitated victim is surrounded by colored beads, seven coins and chicken feathers; ritual sacrifices at wooded sites where black-robed cultists mutilate animals on altars; other homicides where the corpses are found drained of blood with symbols such as a pentagram or inverted cross carved into their chests; drug and pornography rings with nationwide connections to occult groups; carefully executed grave robbing; Satanic rituals and human sacrifices involving children—fantastic stories told by hundreds of children in scores of preschools throughout the United States, all of them relating similar horrors.

I discovered a small clique of police officers—"cult cops" or "ghostbusters" as they're affectionately known by their peers—who have specialized in this field. To their surprise, they find themselves overwhelmed with requests to analyze outside cases and lecture before other law enforcement agencies. The need for this information is growing so quickly that the investigation of occult crime is now being taught in police academies by the same officers who have written the procedural manuals.

This book details the new wave in crime through the eyes of those who are involved in it. But beware: readers who like their crime stories wrapped up with neat conclusions will be disappointed. Occult crimes are rarely solved.

This is new territory, just as drug crimes were in the 1960s, computer crimes in the '70s, and terrorism in the '80s. Most agencies are not yet versed in occult crime investigation, and few cases are examined by experts. I have presented several cases in depth, but the purpose of this book is to show the far-reaching breadth of this type of crime. By my having strung together many incidents, the reader will get a better understanding of occult crime than if he or she read just one or two particular cases. I also have omitted well-known, occult-related crimes like those of Charles Manson and others; enough has been written about these familiar villains. This book will show you crimes in your own neighborhood that you didn't know existed.

Because of the controversy surrounding these crimes, I have chosen to let police officers describe their own experiences. All conversations took place over a two-year period—in some cases I spent several weeks with one particular person—and the interviews were recorded. What you will read are their exact words. All testimony, whenever possible, was corroborated by another investigator, those involved in the crime, police records or court documents. Sometimes several sources were used. Because no one's memory is precise, especially about incidents that occurred many years before, I have occasionally corrected simple errors in dates, times, spelling of names and similar details. Whenever explanations, amplifications, or definitions were necessary, I have set them within brackets. I also have included selected newspaper articles, police reports and official memoranda about incidents to contrast public knowledge with behind-the-scenes knowledge.

You will also read verbatim testimony from those outside the law enforcement community: practitioners of white and black arts, private investigators, doctors, therapists, clergy, victims, and others.

Each investigator has his or her own approach to occult crime, and interpretations may vary from expert to expert. Don't be disturbed if one point of view is followed by a different one. I did not dismiss reliable testimony just because it didn't "fit in." Remember, law enforcement is often more art than science, and this is particularly true of occult crime. Because the field is so new, a consensus on many issues has not been reached by the law enforcement community.

Keep in mind that few who engage in occult activities are criminals. The majority are law-abiding citizens; their activities are considered religions—and are thereby protected under the Constitution. In fact, police find that some of their best sources about occult crimes are those involved in the occult who are eager to rid their own closed communities of the criminal elements.

One final note: it is easy to sensationalize occult crimes by dwelling on gruesome evidence. While I have not omitted anything solely because it is frightening, neither have I included shocking evidence simply to titillate my audience—you won't find any unsupported claims, even from credible sources. But I warn you in advance that there is horrifying material in this book, especially in Chapter 12: The Occult Survivors. Excuse the cliché, but it's not for the squeamish.

There are many people and organizations I would like to thank for their help. Some spent only a short time with me while others spent days and weeks telling me about incidents, introducing me to informants, sharing their notes and showing me evidence from their cases. Some of these people are quoted extensively, while others are not. Even those whose words are not printed here have helped greatly by heading me in the right direction, confirming my sources or by helping me understand the scope of this crime.

Among them are Sgt. Ed Anderson of the San Jose State University Police Department, who shared his research on occult symbols with me; Blanche Barton, administrator of the Church of Satan; Linda Blood, former member of the Temple of Set, who helped me understand more about this particular Satanic cult; Dee Brown, researcher and TV producer, for her insights into preschool cases in Southern California; Sgt. Rod Carpenter of the Contra Costa Sheriff's Office in Martinez, California; Private Investigator Ted Gunderson of Los Angeles, for his contacts in the occult world; Gwyn Gwynallen, Feather, and Margot Adler, practitioners of the occult arts, who taught me the strange beauty of their world; Investigator Judy Hanson; Special Agent Ken Lanning of the FBI Academy Behavioral Sciences Unit in Quantico, Virginia; Father James Le Bar of the New York Archdiocese; Det. P. J. Lawton of the Pima County Sheriff's Department; Police Consultant Jim McCarthy; Tim Maas, Pastoral Counselor, who helped me understand the psychological problems of victims of the occult; Prof. Jeffrey Russell, of the department of history of the University of California at Santa Barbara; Det. Gary Traina of the Newport Beach California Police Department and Dr. Lawrence Pazder, whose compassion for victims of occult crime is enormous.

I would also like to thank Officer Tim Boyle of the Maryland National Capital Park Police, who showed me the action in my own backyard; Det. Jim Bradley of the District of Columbia Metropolitan Police Intelligence Division, who introduced me to the Hispanic occult underworld in the Washington area; Chief Investigator Mike Davison of the Monroe County, Michigan, Sheriff's Office, who shared his most exciting case with me; Capt. Dale Griffis, now retired, of the Tiffin, Ohio,

Police Department, who was more than generous with his time, information and homespun wisdom; Det. Pat Metoyer of the Los Angeles Police Department Criminal Conspiracy Division, whose insights into handling occult crime are unique and painfully practical; Deputy Probation Officer Darlyne Pettinicchio of Orange County, who doesn't give up on teenagers that society has thrown away; Det. Bill Wickersham and his partner Det. Cleo Wilson of the Denver Police Department, whose passion for the subject of occult crime is catching.

More than any other area of criminal activity, occult crime is kept close by police officers, and it took many months for me to gain the trust of investigators.

For help in opening usually closed doors, I especially thank Det. Sandi Gallant of the San Francisco Police Department's Intelligence Division. Because of her excellent reputation in the law enforcement community, mentioning her name got me entrée that I might not have gotten otherwise.

There are also many people whom I cannot name, because they are afraid of retribution from occult groups, humiliated by what happened to them, or because they are police officers whose undercover assignments won't permit their identities to be made public. Additionally, there are police officers who have been told by their departments not to talk about occult crime outside the law enforcement community. Many of them talked with me despite the prohibition, and I thank them for taking the risk. Some of them will recognize their words under the guise of pseudonyms, as we agreed.

Last, I would like to thank my editor Jim Frost for understanding the different turn that this project took and his willingness to embrace it.

Larry Kahaner
Washington, DC
January, 1988

Occult crime may be the most difficult area of police work today. You won't find simple cases with obvious suspects. You find bits and pieces, evidence that goes nowhere, testimony that is always suspect and crimes so bizarre and disgusting that even most police officers don't want to believe it exists.

—DET. SANDI GALLANT,
SAN FRANCISCO POLICE DEPARTMENT

Where all these occult religions go bad is when people aren't satisfied to live within the environment they have created. It's not enough to have power over themselves. They want to control the heavens and each other. As the need for more power grows, occult crime increases. It attracts people who aren't satisfied; they want more power. The more powerful you are, the more people you have power over, and the more powerful you become in turn.

—DET. CLEO WILSON,
DENVER POLICE DEPARTMENT

CHAPTER ONE:

THE CULT COPS

Some police officers are experts in terrorism, gangs, organized crime, or explosives. A handful have focused on occult crime. Some detectives were thrust into the field by a single case, while others have found themselves bewildered by an explosion of apparently bizarre and unrelated cases and have strived to make sense of them. Although each officer approaches the subject in his* own way, each shares an irresistible passion and curiosity about human beings who operate just beyond what most of us would consider the real world.

[Sandi Gallant, forty-four, is a detective with the Intelligence Division of the San Francisco Police Department. In 1972, she made national news by being the first female police officer assigned to street duty in San Francisco. She also worked as the first decoy prostitute, the model for similar police actions now commonplace. Her interest in cults and the occult was triggered by the Jonestown, Guyana, mass suicide of Jim Jones and members of the People's Temple, which was established in San Francisco.]

DET. SANDI GALLANT: I got a call at home on November 23, 1978, from my boss saying, "Do you know anything about People's Temple?"

*The masculine pronoun appears here and elsewhere for simplicity, but should be understood to include both male and female.

I said, "I know they've been right next door to where the Zebra [murders] suspects were for quite some time, and when I worked in Juvenile every once in a while somebody would call and complain that their kid was with this group, but I really know nothing about them." He said, "We're getting reports that two hundred in the group committed suicide."

We both kind of cackled on the phone and said it was ridiculous. Then he said, "But the reports are coming from the State Department." I got serious real fast. "Oh, my. . . ." And he said, "Well, I just wanted to know if you knew anything about it."

By the next day, the count was four hundred people. The Department had somebody who was working with the FBI, but the information wasn't being gathered fast enough. I was working prison gangs at the time, eating my lunch one day in the office, and the boss said "Daly, get in here! [Daly was Gallant's maiden name.] I got an assignment for you. The FBI needs someone to work liaison, to gather information, put files together." I've always been fairly good at putting systems together, so I said, "Okay." [Before entering the police academy, Gallant worked as a civilian employee in the Police Department. She compiled the Department's first comprehensive tattoo and scar file as well as a left- and right-handed file of criminals.]

What I did mostly was a lot of paper shuffling, a lot of paper handling. I wasn't directly involved in the interviews until later on. One of the fellows in our office, however, Don Daniels, did some interviews of the survivors when they came back. One of the janitors in our building lost his wife and five children. Don and I did that interview, which was tough. A little bit after that, less than a year later, the man who was to become my partner, Jerry Belfield, and I got involved with some of the survivors who were living over in the East Bay.

Jeannie Mills, who was an ex-member of People's Temple, was murdered along with her husband in their home in Berkeley. Their daughter was critically wounded. [Mills and her husband Al ran a halfway house for former cult members called the Human Freedom Center.] The original call came from one of the Jonestown survivors who was living over in Berkeley, and our immediate thought was, Oh my God, someone from the Temple killed them. It's starting again, but that turned out not to be the case.

We began doing some surveillance on some of Jones's adopted children, just to get a feel for whether they were a little agitated or too excited, while Berkeley [Police Department] was trying to put the case together. That was really the beginning of how we got involved in cults. As it turned out, the D.A. didn't have enough to go to prosecution, but the investigation suggested that the son had shot the parents and critically wounded his sister.

Out of that, over a period of months working that case, we developed a general interest in the area of cults. I eventually went back in to the boss and said, "There are other groups out there, certainly not to the point where the Jones group was, but there are some concerns around." I told him that I didn't necessarily look at law enforcement as something that always reacts after something happens but before it happens. I reminded him that our Department was starting to receive a series of complaints regarding specific organizations, and perhaps it might be wise to give it some serious thought.

Murphy, the boss, said, "Go for it," which was highly unusual, because you have a problem. You have the First Amendment, freedom of religion, so I made it very clear to him that I wasn't going in looking at the ideology of groups but their actions. I think the reason why they let us go ahead with this was People's Temple. We got caught with our pants down.

[Dale Griffis, fifty, was captain of the Tiffin, Ohio, Police Department. Before his retirement in 1986, he served the

Department for twenty-six years. His father was a sergeant with the Tiffin police, and he retired on the same day that his son, Dale, joined. Griffis is now a private consultant to law enforcement agencies on occult crime. He receives up to twenty-five inquiries daily and about a foot of mail weekly. He even has received mail addressed only "Cult Cop, Ohio." His interest in cults and the occult began with a bizarre suicide in a neighboring town.]

CAPT. DALE GRIFFIS: There was a case here, just down the road from Tiffin, where a fifteen-year-old had committed suicide. The young boy had become quite enamored with occult activity. He was found in a garage, with occult writings all over his body. He was between two black candles. The police chief was under a lot of pressure. Why did this happen?—upper-class parents and so on. The chief said to me, "Dale, you've got a degree in psychology and all that, so why don't you take a look; we've got a hell of a problem."

EXCERPT OF MEMO FROM WILLARD POLICE DEPARTMENT TO PROJECT INFO MEMBERS
[a regional police intelligence group]:

On 23 March 1980 the fifteen-year-old son of a local official committed suicide by hanging himself in the loft of the residential garage. The deceased was found by a family member at about 0700 hours on 24 March. The youth had covered himself with curious writings that give the appearance of being inspired by cultish connections referencing Satanic origins. Descriptions of markings as follows:

Upper torso, below base of neck, "Satan" printed w/orange lipstick.

Middle of torso (chest), "IM COME HOME MASTER" [*sic*] printed with ballpoint pen.

Middle lung area, the numbers "666" printed with orange lipstick.

Left ribcage area, "SATAN" printed w/orange lipstick.

Front of right leg and ankle, "I LOVE SATAN" w/ ballpoint pen.

Buttock area, vertical line and, crosswise across top of the buttocks, a horizontal line at the bottom of the vertical line. These lines have the appearance of an upside down cross when viewed from top to bottom; this was done w/orange lipstick.

Inside of left thigh, "LUCIFER" printed w/orange lipstick. Blood analysis indicated there was no drugs or toxins present.

CAPT. DALE GRIFFIS: By the time I got there the crime scene had been disturbed. I talked with the investigators; I tried the parents. I wanted to know what kind of things the kid was reading. I guess I was looking for the psychological reason at the time, approaching it from a pseudoscientific angle. I couldn't get much from the parents. They were in no condition to talk about it. The investigators were pretty much certain that it wasn't a murder. I was bothered by the writing being in hard to reach places on his body, but I also knew that a distorted mind can be devious and creative.

I drove over with the chief of our department, and on the way back I said, "I don't know, Dave, I've got a lot of questions in the back of my mind that have got to be settled. I think what bothers me more than anything else is that I think this type of activity is going to become worse in the United States."

It wasn't a scientific wild-ass guess. I guess I had been boot smart from school. Keep in mind that I had been taught the transition of the modality of criminals and all that psychological mumbo jumbo, but I had police experience going back forty years at that time. When you're born into the cop business and it's in your blood . . . there's something from my roots and everything else that said there's a problem. Take all that and something inside of me says there's something here. Call it a hunch or whatever you want.

The questions kept on my mind. I asked Tom Spellerberg, the local prosecutor. "Tom, maybe I'm all wrong, but we've got some of these groups floating around in America that very few people know anything about. One of these days, you're really going to have to do something. Nobody's doing anything, no type of study, nothing. You've got FOJ funds [local Furtherance of Justice funds]. If I guarantee you not to leave law enforcement and use what I learn to help the citizens of Seneca County, would you see that I get some training?" He said, "Where would you go to school?" I said, "By God that's a good question."

[Pat Metoyer, forty-seven, a twenty-two-year veteran of the Los Angeles Police Department, is currently a member of the Criminal Conspiracy Section. He has worked in juvenile and homicide departments. His interest in the occult is an outgrowth of his investigations into brainwashing by cult groups.]

DET. PAT METOYER: When I was in the public disorder intelligence division we monitored groups. Some of the groups we monitored were Scientology as well as some of the other religious groups. You begin to see that in some of those organizations there's a certain amount of brainwashing that must necessarily take place in order for a person to believe. A good example of that is Jim Jones and the People's Temple. Of that whole group, the dumbest person there was the last one to drink the poison. He saw all his friends drink this stuff and go belly up, and he stood in line to get a drink of this damn poison. That shows you the power of brainwashing, and I began doing some studies with respect to brainwashing, number one, and as they related to cults, number two. I wanted to learn how to pick out those persons who would be most susceptible to cult involvements.

About four or five years ago, I was lecturing about nationalistic terrorism. The fellow in charge of a seminar asked me, "Would you like to lecture for me at an exposition for law enforcement officers?" I said "Sure," but he says, "Instead of talking about nationalistic terrorism how about religious terrorism?" I said, "No way, I wouldn't do that."

He persisted. "I really would like to have you lecture, but I'd like to have something that has some links with religion." I finally said, "Okay, how about if I do my research and I lecture on Satanism and the occult?" He said "Okay."

[Bill Wickersham, thirty-seven, is a detective with the Denver Police Department. His father was a sheriff and encouraged Bill to become a police officer. Wickersham's special interest in the occult came about as the result of an investigation into a juvenile prostitution ring. His partner was Det. Cleo Wilson.]

DET. BILL WICKERSHAM: All we did that summer was ride around in the patrol car, my partner Cleo and me. We got right into the line of cars [picking up male prostitutes], and by the time we got around the right corner we would find somebody new, some kid that we hadn't seen before. We asked for I.D., that sort of thing. The first week we had twelve complaints of harassment. I mean we were busy.

We got in good with some of the adult male hookers. They snitched on the kids because they were ruining their business.

One night we got a complaint that some juvenile prostitutes were hanging out at a sandwich place at 13th and Grand

Avenue, in the Capital Hill area of Denver. They were supposed to be runaways. We interviewed them and knew they were runaways because they all told different stories. We brought them downtown. Four kids total.

We found out that three were runaways. The oldest boy said he was eighteen, but we couldn't verify it so we had to let him go. It turned out later he was only seventeen, a juvenile. The other kids were either sent to shelters or their parents picked them up.

We had been noticing that many of the juveniles we picked up had insignias on their jackets and clothes—inverted crosses and "666." I remember one kid we picked up for dope had a great big inverted cross on the back of his jacket. Above that he had an inverted pentagram, and below the cross he had "666." Not only that, but he had calling cards with all these symbols on it and the type of sex he would perform. It just blew my mind.

I said to Cleo, "This son of a bitch is evil." I know what "666" means, and I know what the inverted cross means. I knew the "666" from the Bible, and I knew from catechism that the inverted cross was the symbol of the Antichrist.

I saw it with this doper we picked up, and now we were seeing it with these other kids we had. Not only that, but one kid's father started telling us stories about how the kids were into witchcraft and I said, "What kind of bullshit . . ." He said, "I have a whole box of stuff that one of the kids left at my house." I said, "What have you got?" and he described all this crazy stuff, and I looked at Cleo and said, "Oh, shit, what is going on here?"

He brought in the box the next day, and it had inverted crosses, pentagrams, athames [ceremonial daggers], pacts with Satan that these kids had written. I said to Cleo, "This is evil. This is *Exorcist* shit." That movie scared the living piss out of me. Being a Catholic it scared me.

The father was anxious to know about his son's younger

brother. He was ten years old, and the father didn't know where he was. We started asking the kids about him, but we couldn't talk to them. They were in another world. They spoke a different language.

[Cleo (short for Cleotilde) Wilson, forty, has been a police officer for thirteen years with the Denver Police Department. She and Bill Wickersham became partners about seven years ago.]

DET. CLEO WILSON: Talking to this group of kids was probably the hardest thing we had ever done. We had talked to other kids, prostitutes, kids who are victims of violence, but we never had so many problems getting information as we did with these kids. They lied for each other constantly. They were hard as rocks. There was no conscience.

We had a ten-year-old out there, and we would do almost anything to get to him. We didn't know if they had leased him out to some john or what.

We finally found out where he was. He was in a hotel on East Colfax in a high crime area. We found a sixteen-year-old girl with him.

It was kind of an eerie feeling to see these kids who were so hardcore, and seeing the kinds of things they had pledged—pacts with Satan, pledges of fidelity to the group.

We needed to know about the older kid, the one that everyone else was protecting. His name was Donald Bradley. We figured he was the leader.

EXCERPT FROM THE DIARY OF DONALD BRADLEY
[Some additional letters have been added by Bradley to make the words pronounceable but there are misspellings, too.]

SDRAWKCAB REYARP SDROL
LORD'S PRAYER BACKWARDS

NEMA LIVEE MORF SU REVILLED TUB
NOISHAYTPMET OOTNI TON SUH DEEL
SUH TSHAIGA SAPJERT TATH YETH
VIGRAWF WZA SESAPSERT RUA SUH VIGRAWF
DERB ILAID RUA YED SITH SUH VIG
NEVAH NI SI ZA THRE NI
NUB EEB LIW EIB EYTH
MAIN EYTH EB DWOHLAH
NEVEH NITRA CHIOO
REHTAF RUO!

　　When through with the Lord's prayer backwards, blow out the candle and say "So mote it be."

DET. CLEO WILSON: I had been brought up in a strict Catholic background. I knew about the devil and demonic possession, so I was aware of the symbolism. I knew what they meant, but I didn't know if they were meaning the same things to these kids as what I had been taught.

So, we went to a priest at the high school where I had been and talked to him. He referred us to Jim McCarthy, an instructor at the University at Boulder. He went to juvenile hall with us and asked them questions in vernacular that they could understand. We sat there and realized why we weren't getting anywhere. We didn't even speak the same language.

After a while, we were able to piece together information about this group, what they were doing and who was in charge. Bill and I both had trouble believing what we were hearing.

CHAPTER TWO:

THE EDUCATION

Only a few years ago, occult investigators had no law enforcement manuals to guide them. They found themselves reading books about religion, witchcraft and Satanism and talking to clergymen, college professors and those who practiced the occult arts.

Confronted by crimes that didn't have the usual motives or leave the usual evidence patterns, officers relied mostly on each other for support and information. Many were part of an informal network, a clique of cops who still weren't sure what they were looking at but who took comfort in the fact that other agencies were seeing the same crimes. Eventually, they wrote the manuals themselves. Information and investigation techniques were passed around on mimeographed pages and through lectures.

Little by little they developed a legitimate area of law enforcement study. More important, they confirmed for themselves something many of them still didn't believe or want to believe: Bizarre crimes, related to ancient occult teachings, actually were taking place in the twentieth century.

DET. SANDI GALLANT: I was looking for anyone who knew anything about cult matters as it related to law enforcement. I remember having a conversation with Dale Griffis, who was working cults to some extent. He was the police captain in Tiffin, Ohio, at the time. Dale asked if we had started looking at any occult groups and not just cult groups. I said we had been looking mainly at cults like the Moonies, the Rastafarians, the Hare Krishnas. There had been allegations some members had been involved in drugs, guns, kidnaping. Some were substantiated and some weren't. Dale said that maybe we should be looking at the occult groups as well. I told him I was always interested in something new and that we had been hearing some things that sounded like they might be occult related. I told him that my partner and I were interested, but we never seemed to have the time to do the investigations that we wanted. They kept us pretty busy.

We had been doing some networking with other agencies throughout the country besides Dale and also with some agencies in Canada about occult groups. Slowly, we began to hear stories about occult activity. We decided to send out some inquiries over the teletype just to see if other departments were seeing the same things. Looking back now at it, we were pretty naive at the time about the material and the way we worded the message, but the responses we got were interesting. It showed us that we were on the right track. Something was going on out there. Other departments had taken notice, but nobody knew exactly what to make of it.

REQUEST FOR NATIONWIDE BROADCAST
018/SAN FRANCISCO PD/CA
ATTN: INTELLIGENCE AND HOMICIDE DIVISIONS

THIS DEPARTMENT IS CURRENTLY CONDUCTING
INVESTIGATIONS INTO SATANIC CULTS WHICH
MAY BE INVOLVED IN ANIMAL MUTILATIONS AND
RITUALISTIC HOMICIDES OF HUMAN BEINGS,
WHEREIN INTERNAL ORGANS ARE REMOVED
FROM THE VICTIMS AND USED IN CHURCH BAP-
TISMS AND RITUALS.

WE ARE ALSO INTERESTED IN SUSPICIOUS DEATHS WHEREIN THE VICTIM WAS BELIEVED TO BE INVOLVED IN CULT ACTIVITIES. THIS PARTICULAR GROUP IS KNOWN TO TRAVEL THROUGHOUT THE COUNTRY IN SMALL BANDS OF 10-15 PEOPLE, EITHER BY FOOT OR IN VANS AND WAGONS. THEY PREY ON YOUNG ADULTS 15-30 YEARS.

ANY INFORMATION FORWARD TO OFFICER SANDI DALY, SAN FRANCISCO POLICE INTELLIGENCE DIVISION.

[Oct. 10, 1980]

NOTES OF RESPONSES

Eugene, Oregon PD: WMA [White Male Adult] 18 advises he was approached in a shopping mall by a group called The Gray Witches. They wanted him to go to Colorado. Allegedly the group was involved in animal mutilations, and they were talking about human sacrifices.

Brentwood, Tenn. PD: Devil worshipers were in their area 9/23. Known to sacrifice dogs and cats. 3 years ago several dogs and cats missing—throats cut. Used a church in Nashville.

Iowa Division of Criminal Investigation: Has been investigating Satanic groups. 1974-75, numerous animal mutilations; Sept. '79 to Dec. '79, nine mutilations—eyes, ears, tongues and reproductive organs are removed. If ears are damaged they don't remove them. Sharp instrument is used. Injection marks in jugular veins. Allegedly ketamine given before sacrifice. [Ketamine hydrochloride is an anesthetic that can produce catatonia.]

Los Angeles, PD: Group called *Santeria* [Spanish for "worship of saints," a mixture of African tribal religion and Catholicism. More on *Santeria* and other Hispanic occult religions in Chapter 7] involved in ritualistic animal mutilations. Members advocate human sacrifices however the high priest says not at this time.

New Mexico State Police: Has been investigating animal mutilations for four years. Believes aircraft of some type used. Blood is drawn out through jugular vein. Cow's own heart used as pump.

DET. SANDI GALLANT: Around this same time we got an anonymous call from someone who said they had information that there was going to be a human sacrifice at a motel in the Fisherman's Wharf area.

At the same time that we got this, which sounded very crazy, police in Vancouver, British Columbia, got similar reports. It was almost like you wanted to blow it all off, but you can't because you never know whether a piece of information is true or not. The caller didn't say when this would occur, but we just assumed Halloween—the occult, spirits, and so forth. We didn't know any better. We couldn't develop anything further on the alleged sacrifice, but we kept hearing the same sorts of things from other agencies.

We decided that we better do some checking around, so we started with the public library. We just began reading everything we could. We learned about some of the significant occult holidays and started doing surveillance on those dates.

We did what I see a lot of other cops doing. We hear about something occult and we automatically think Satanic. As it turns out, a group we were getting information about was called OTO [*Ordo Templi Orientis;* more on them in Chapter 4], a pagan group that follows the teachings of Aleister Crowley, who some look upon as the Beast himself. They're probably a very Satanically oriented group but not Satanic in the true sense if you were to ask contemporary Satanic groups. OTO is looked down upon by many Satanic groups who don't want much to do with them.

We found out where they were in Berkeley, and we drove over to see what was going on. We found out from the calendar of events that only one night is an open ritual. We discovered that everything the OTO does is "skyclad," which means naked. Well, you're not going to get me in there, but Jerry says, "I am ready, just send me in the door." Needless to say we didn't go, but we sat outside to see what was going on.

Near the building, we ran into Chief Murphy who said, "What are you two doing working on a Sunday?" I said, "We're going to go over there and watch a bunch of witches do their thing." He just laughed and said, "You guys are crazy. You really believe in this stuff, don't you?" I said, "Well, somebody's out there doing something. We're interested in seeing what it is they do." He goes, "You know, you're not going to be happy until you get a homicide, are you?" We just kind of laughed and did our surveillance.

Well, we didn't see much. We saw them walk from a dilapidated house next door to the church in their white robes. The only thing we saw was them holding something about the size of a basketball covered with a white sheet and carry it into the church. We sat there all night long in the pouring rain for nothing, absolutely nothing.

I got home about eleven o'clock, turned on the TV news and there was our coroner, Boyd Stephens, who says something to the effect that "This is a ritualistic homicide." I said to myself, uh, oh. I called Jerry and told him to put on the TV. I said, "There was a homicide in Golden Gate Park; the victim was beheaded, and there were chicken feathers stuck in the neck. I think we can expect internal affairs to pay us a visit in the morning, Jerry. We'll probably be the suspects.

Remember the chief's last remarks about how we wouldn't be happy. . . ."

The next morning we got called down to the bureau of inspectors, and they gave us the details of the homicide.

EXCERPT OF SAN FRANCISCO POLICE DEPARTMENT INCIDENT REPORT # 81165801

Date and Time Reported to Police: 2-8-81, 1210
Location of Occurrence: Golden Gate Pk, "Alvord Lake"
Reporting Officer: J. Dougherty
Victim: John Doe #12, Race: N, Sex: M, Residence: Unk, DOB [date of birth] or Age: Unk.
Witness 1 and Witness 2 responded to the officer approx. 1210 hours this date to report on someone sleeping in Golden Gate Park. This R/O [responding officer] responded with W1 and W2 to area just south of Alvord Lake and near the wooden steps found a blue sleeping bag in the bushes with someone in it. Upon further investigation and by using my baton to lift the loose sleeping bag, I discovered a complete decapitation. At the area where the head should have been was a chicken wing. Also present were two kernels of corn. R/O requested Hudelson and Sgt. Rhodes who in turn requested assistance of coroners T. Leader, J. Beaver and homicide inspectors Hendrix and Byrne. Photo lab inspector Cashen responded for photos. Insp. Dubor of crime lab responded to take physical evidence. Human head not located. Body of chicken found by Sgt. Landman approx. 50 yds from corpse in south westerly direction. Chief medical ex-

aminer Stephens took charge of investigation. M.
Parto/J. Morluck secured area and kept spectators
away during investigation.

DET. SANDI GALLANT: They're laying this stuff out for us
and Jerry and I are looking at one another. We didn't want to
appear real stupid so I said, "Yeah, looks like *Santeria* to me."
But really we didn't know much about it. We told them we
were interested in pursuing it further.

We spent the next several days trying to grab everything
we could about it. We spoke to Charles Wetli, the coroner in
Dade County [Florida] who is the national expert on *Santeria*,
ran it by him, and he said it sounded right. There were supposed to be coins in multiples of seven, but we didn't find any
of that. He explained to us about the corn kernels.

MEMO
TO: OFFICER DALY
Officer Daly: Fried corn is sometimes used as pay-
ment to the [*Santeria*] god Eleggua!
C. WETLI, M.D. 2/13/81.

DET. SANDI GALLANT: Around the same time, a fireman
had phoned our office. He told us about a call a week ago in
Golden Gate Park—not near the decapitation incident. There
was a bonfire with a bunch of people standing around with
painted faces, robes, and there was a circle with what was
described as a pentagram made out of string on the ground.
There were dogs sitting around the area. They called the police, and the people began dispersing. The officer called for
backup. They talked to one of the people, and all he said was
that they were exercising their freedom of religion. That was
the end of it. No report was made.

We tried to follow up. The coroner went out to the scene

with us, and he found a cardboard box with the carcasses of dead chickens. It was maggoted. We of course passed that information along to homicide, but there was nothing to indicate any connection with the decapitation. We had learned that someone totally involved in *Brujeria* [Spanish for witchcraft with roots in Latin America] or *Santeria*—what we thought had been involved in the dead man's case—would not use the pentagram. It's a totally different thing.

We spent many more days learning everything we could about *Santeria*, black magic, the occult, witchcraft, Satanism, and we put together a ten-page report and sent it down to homicide. In the report we broke down what we thought might have transpired, in general terms, what they would have done with the head: bury it for twenty-one days and during another twenty-one-day period maybe even sleep with it and so on. It culminates with a forty-two-day period after which any power that you can derive from the spirit of this person is over. After that, you discard it. Of course, homicide laughed at us. They thought we were nuts. They would make chicken jokes when we passed by and all that sort of stuff.

So we went about our business and a few weeks later the homicide investigator, Mike Byrne, gets a call at home. They had found the head of a black man not too far from where the body was found. Mike told me that as he was driving into the city he was thinking how long it had been since the incident had happened. It seemed like it was about six weeks. It turned out to be forty-two days right on the money. I don't want to say that Mike had become a believer, but when anyone called him about anything like this, he passed it on. He gave a lot more credibility to it. I go back with Mike a long time; he's a real good Catholic boy, and I think this scared the crap out of him.

What frustrated me so much was that it was easy to bad-mouth homicide and say, why weren't you staking out the park on the forty-second day? But we weren't there either. We can kiss it off and say, well, we're an information gathering unit, and our job [in the Intelligence Division] is just to pass information on to you. But if Jerry and I really believed it we should have been there, and we weren't.

[The dead man was later identified as Leroy Carter, age twenty-nine, who had a history of criminal activity including arrests for auto theft, assault and battery, and trespassing. His murder remains unsolved.]

CAPT. DALE GRIFFIS: Tom Spellerberg, our prosecutor, was highly supportive. I brought up the Willard suicide and some other things, too. I said we knew that some of these cult groups were stealing a lot of money. We really didn't know a hell of a lot about them, and whatever it was that these non-traditional groups, as I began to call them, were doing, we needed to know about it.

I had been talking to Sandi by phone for a while because she knew about the Jonestown thing. I had gotten the FOJ funds and travelled to California. Sandi met me at the airport in San Francisco, and we spent some time together. My impression was that she's obviously a very sensitive woman hidden behind a glockenspiel of police armament. She's all heart. I found her to be a good police officer.

We went into the Wicked Eye bookstore; she had never been in there. The girl behind the counter had a "666" tattooed on one boob and an upside down cross on the other. Real first class.

We drove by Anton LaVey's house. [Anton LaVey is the founder of the Church of Satan and author of *The Satanic Bible*.] We went to the botanicas of the *Santerians*. [Botanicas sell herbs, powders, and other paraphernalia used in *Santeria* rituals.] I went out on the pier and tried to be recruited by the Moonies. I listened to their spiel. We tried to soak up as much as we could, bouncing ideas off each other.

I had heard about the Book of Shadows, but it didn't mean diddly shit to me. I didn't know what it was. Sandi and I found one in the occult shop and looked at it. The Book of Shadows is what occultists use to write their personal prayers and incantations to summon the demons. It's a diary of occult activity, with blank pages that you fill in, but we didn't know that at the time. We looked at this thing in the store and said, "Boy, this thing's a gyp. It's got no writing in it." Afterwards we laughed about it.

Sandi knew more about the subject than I did. She had been there before me. She earned my respect. I liked her stable approach. She didn't jump off the barn roof as I had seen done.

During my trip, I had become more convinced that my hunch was correct, that this stuff was out there. Before I saw Sandi, I had spent about a week in Southern California. I have a great respect for LAPD, but I was bothered by the way they had handled some of the Manson stuff. They were treating it like an isolated incident, and it wasn't.

I had five days in Southern California and five days with Sandi, and then my money was up. I came back and debriefed Spellerberg and some other people. Basically I said, "We ain't seen nothing yet."

Their reaction? They were surprised. Here we are in this little niche of suburbia, and I was telling them about the Moonies and *Santeria*, and they thought, Jesus, this guy is nuts.

I was starting to have some physical problems from a high school football injury coupled with a car accident that occurred while I was on the force. A doctor in Columbus told me I would be out for about six months with leg surgery. I decided that I didn't want the down time, so I looked for a college that would allow me to research this topic and get some academic credit while I was on sick leave.

I checked and found Columbia Pacific University in San Rafael and talked to them, told them what I wanted to do, and they were really nice to me. I had written a manual for my Master's degree on criminal investigation guidelines. My final Ph.D. dissertation expanded on some of that. It was called "Mind Control Cults and Their Effects on the Objectives of Law Enforcement." I stayed in Tiffin and spent a couple of thousand dollars on mail and telephone to do the research.

What I did had never been done before. I polled former cult members about their activities. I sent out five hundred questionnaires. The data I came up with was startling. It said, basically, that these people were killers who would do almost anything the leader said.

EXCERPT FROM "MIND CONTROL CULTS AND THEIR EFFECTS ON THE OBJECTIVES OF LAW ENFORCEMENT"

If the TOP leader of the group came to you personally which of the following would you honor?

sell drugs—26%
work free—94%
rob a store—20%
steal food—32%
plant a bomb—14%
shoot a non-believer—34%

CAPT. DALE GRIFFIS: No one had ever done this before. It was all new. It gave law enforcement an idea of what they were up against. I had been running Project Info, a seventy-five-agency group of police departments that shared information in Northwest Ohio and surrounding area. My dissertation data was shared among this group, and as time went on I got some reports of cult activity. The Willard suicide had already happened. The members knew about that, but we were starting to see a lot of other things. I was laying low, to tell you the truth, just gathering information, sifting it. I had trouble believing a lot of what I heard and was hesitant about passing it on.

In the fall of 1981, we needed money for Project Info, so we decided to hold a seminar. We charged some very low rate, like $50 for a three-day seminar. One of the speakers was going to be an hour late, and I was the emcee. Someone asked me to fill in, to talk about some of the things I had learned in California. I said, "I don't know if you guys are ready for this or not. I've never given a lecture before about this subject." But I did the talk anyway. I spoke for one solid hour about cults and the occult. I just sort of covered the topic with little bits and pieces, just as a teaser, and people came to me afterwards and said, "Where did you get that weird stuff from?" It blew them away. I never realized there was so much interest among law enforcement people about this subject.

From then on I was off. I would get calls from police who had problems in this area. I suppose these things had been going on for quite some time, but police never had anyone they could tell it to before because the stuff was too weird, too bizarre. The calls would often begin, "I know that you're not going to believe this, Dale, but here's what our deputies found in the woods. . . ."

DET. PAT METOYER: I am a great reader. I usually read three to four hours a day. This subject fascinates me. I try to learn as much as I can by reading and talking to people.

I went to Dr. Reiser, our police psychiatrist. I wanted to know if anyone in the mental health field had done a study on Satanism and Witchcraft. He said, "No, not really." I tried to find anyone at Stanford or UCLA to see if they did any studies on how it impacts the family. You're leading two lives, after all. In the group they're eager to embrace Satan, but you don't find too many people in the street saying, "I'm a Satan worshiper." They'll say, "I'm a Catholic, I'm a Jew, I'm a Protestant," but you won't find anybody saying "I'm a Satanist," so it's really got to impact somebody's life.

Reiser told me that as far as he knew there were no studies about Satanism, meaning the worship of Satan or demons, and I thought that was kind of strange. I thought maybe we were a little late. It was 1985, and these cases had already begun to surface.

I had started lecturing on occult topics to police officers. Basically, I helped policemen identify what is occult activity —what it is and how it originates. So few people in police circles knew anything about this topic that I started getting calls from around the country.

Here was my first case:

I got this call one day from a police officer. He says he has a female who has a nine-year-old daughter. She, the woman, has now remarried. Her current spouse has taken the daughter to visit his parents in Florida. When he gets to Florida—the mother stays behind because she's still working—he takes the daughter to his father and mother's farm. In fact, there's no one there; it's just a large barn. The little girl says that when they get there, there are all these men. At least she thinks they're men; they're dressed like sheiks. Some kind of flowing garments, and they have a hat or hood.

In this barn she remembers animals, stuffed heads. So Dad says, "Gosh, they'd like to see you dance. Why don't you dance for them?"

The girl said she danced for these people, and they were clapping. She said there were three fires, not one. She began dancing around the fires. Then Dad says, "You know, you must be getting really hot. Why don't you take off your clothes. You would be cool."

She does what her stepfather says, and continues to dance. Then Dad says, "Why don't you sit on my lap"—this is all what the mother is reporting to the police who then referred the case to me—and she does, and the dad takes a knife or razor blade and makes a small incision in her vagina. He takes blood and puts it in a vial. He asks her to dance some more and says that the cut will only sting a little bit, and he will kiss and make it better. With that, all the other men began dancing again. After a while, she put her clothes back on. Later on the stepfather and she went back to the motel.

The cop said to me, "What do you think we have?"

I said, "A bunch of goddamn pedophiles."

He said, "Well, what about the hoods and all that?"

I told him to look at the scene. You have three fires. Right off the bat I can tell you that you're not dealing with witches, because witches would have a single fire. They're trying to generate their power into one area; why divide your power?

I asked him to ask the girl about the robes, and it turns out they were all different. There was no uniformity, except that they were all men. There was no real bleeding. It wasn't "blood of the month," which witches use for casting spells. And when Dad says, "I'll kiss it and make it better," that's kind of a key, a tip-off of something else. . . .

I told the cop it wasn't witchcraft, and it had nothing to do with any Satanic or demonic activity, because there was no altar. In the end, he called back and told me that mother hadn't given him all the information. Her husband had been a little kinky in the past. Among other things, he liked having intercourse during her period, smearing the blood on her belly, that sort of thing. I told him, "You got some deviant. He wasn't into the occult."

[Some police officers find that those outside the law enforcement community, especially academics with a background in religious history, are helpful.]

DENVER POLICE DEPARTMENT, SUPPLEMENTARY REPORT, CASE #776126

9-3-82. Officers Wickersham and Wilson contacted a Jim McCarthy, who is an expert on cults.

9-4-82. Mr. Jim McCarthy responded to police headquarters and witnessed interview with Donald Bradley 10:45 A.M. in juvenile hall. Officers advised Bradley of his rights in presence of Maureen A. Cain (Office of the Public Defender). Both the attorney and Bradley gave permission for McCarthy to be present. McCarthy questioned Bradley about the cults and asked if he was the coven leader. Bradley stated that he was but that he had learned all his Witchcraft from David Goldman. McCarthy asked how many were in his cult. Bradley answered seven.

[Jim McCarthy has a master's degree in theology and comparative religions. He has worked at the Institute for the Study of New Religious Movements, in Berkeley. He founded Sanctuary, Inc., a group that provided information about cults to the public.]

JIM MCCARTHY: I had been working as a consultant, researcher, and lecturer in the area of deviant social behavior, which includes a lot of different types of cases going back ten years. Prior to the last three or four years I had calls every couple of months about the occult. Since that time it has increased about one hundred percent or more every year.

The William Acree case was an instance involving male prostitution where the social bonding mechanism was Satanism. Satanism and the symbols provided the cohesiveness and boundary marking mechanism for that group. What I did was explain to Bill and Cleo how Satanism served as a mechanism for these kids.

There was a ten-year-old who was told that if he gave information to the authorities Satan would know and set him on fire while he slept. The kid was eventually found in a hotel room with cuts and bruises all over him because he had been sold to johns.

Something that Bill and Cleo had to recognize is just how powerful those symbols were, especially with adolescents. Fear was the mechanism, but the particular form which it took was Satanism. The boy was told to perform certain acts and bring back money because if he didn't the group, psychically, would know. Satan would know.

Once Donald Bradley realized that he couldn't bullshit Bill and Cleo, he came clean. He seemed physically shaken and in some sense felt victimized himself by Satan. Maybe that was part of an act. I don't know, but I don't think so. He was frightened and asked for protection. He wanted protection from a holy man like a priest or perhaps a medicine man because he was an American Indian.

The follow-up to Goldman is that he moved in with a "Tough Love" family after his father committed suicide and his mother couldn't handle him any longer. I spoke to him afterwards about doing something creative with his life, perhaps going back to his own religion which was Jewish, instead of continuing with Satanism. He was a very hard nut, as much as anybody I've ever met. He was addicted to power.

DET. CLEO WILSON: Through Jim McCarthy we were beginning to learn about this group of kids we brought in and the occult in general. Jim had asked one of the kids about the Book of Shadows. That was a new one on us. By looking at the Book of Shadows, McCarthy learned about the group's inner workings.

As it turned out there was a conflict between the older boy, the seventeen-year-old, and Goldman, who was two years younger. The younger boy had more knowledge of the occult, but the older one was more charismatic, and he became the self-appointed leader or high priest.

At the same time, we're beginning to go to classes that McCarthy is teaching and he keeps giving us books to read. We're also reading books that the father had brought in. It's a lot of Witchcraft, but there was also a *Necronomicon* [Book of the Dead] and a *Satanic Bible*.

The case went on for a long time. It was very confusing because of all the players and the strange circumstances. The case didn't end with these kids. They said they had been turning tricks for the head of a halfway house, William Acree. We never prosecuted the kids, but we did get the head of the halfway house.

DET. BILL WICKERSHAM: We believed that William Acree, the head of the halfway house, had used the older boy, seventeen-year-old Don Bradley, to control the kids into turning tricks. Bradley used the occult group, his own power and knowledge, to control the kids for Acree. Bradley believed he had power and the kids believed it too.

DET. CLEO WILSON: We kept asking each other how come nobody in law enforcement knows about this stuff. Why can't we go to someone? We went to the occult shops and tried to learn as much as we could, but they were as secretive as the kids. We didn't know the right questions to ask. As we got bolder, we went in dressed in uniform. Some treated us like the plague; others spoke to us but were real careful what they said.

Our immediate supervisor was very open to us looking into this area. The lieutenant kind of went along with it but wasn't real happy. The people in our particular unit weren't real happy about what we were doing either. They called us "shit magnets," because anything that became real cruddy we ended up finding or doing.

It was kind of strange because we started getting calls almost immediately from cops asking us things about Satanism. I couldn't believe it because at this time we had just read a lot of books, gone to the classes, and worked this one case. At the time I remember thinking, what are they doing calling us? We don't know any more than they do.

It was clear to us that police all over the country were seeing these sorts of cases, more than anyone would have believed. I had no idea our name was getting around, and it caused a lot of trouble in our own department for us.

CHAPTER THREE:

THE HEAT

Fighting occult crime is only part of the battle for police officers. The other part is fighting the establishment. Some officers find themselves confronting skepticism in their own department when the cases appear.

Some take it hard, vowing to stop taking occult cases because it's not worth the heartache. Others become more steadfast, hoping to convince their superiors of the need for such investigations by doing the most professional work possible. Still others take it philosophically, realizing that anything new will always be suspect. They take solace in stories about the early days of organized crime. Despite growing evidence, some higher-ups then didn't trust the unbelievable stories told by foot patrolmen and detectives about citywide and nationwide crime families with locks on gambling, prostitution, drugs, and infiltration of legitimate businesses.

[Ray Parker is the pseudonym of a detective working for a Northern California county. He asked that his name not be used because his agency does not permit its officers to speak to the media about occult crime.]

DET. RAY PARKER: Probably the biggest problem is what we call "The Heat." Occult crime is a sensitive subject, one that needs to be looked into, but one that you have to walk a fine line. If you were to ask me on the record about occult crime, my answer would be that we don't have that sort of thing in our county. Our county officials don't want it publicized, and we have to go along with it. That's pretty amazing considering our county probably has one of the most active occult populations in California.

You get tired sometimes of the harassment and apathy from your superiors because many of the cases you work on amount to nothing—just bits and pieces of things. Unlike other investigations, few of these cases ever get wrapped up in a neat little package and shipped off to the DA for prosecution.

The stuff you hear about is so bizarre and so out of the realm of police work that when you tell your colleagues about it they think you're nuts. Every so often, we just have to pull back and work on cases in other areas.

DET. BILL WICKERSHAM: We had an incident where a sixteen-year-old boy committed suicide. He was into Satanism and drugs. There's always drugs. After the case, I told my sergeant that we really better start looking into this area. We, as a police department, better have someone who knows about this in case this sort of thing ever comes up again.

He was all for it and said to go ahead with it, but some of the higher-ups thought we were loony bins. They thought we were really off our rockers. The comment was, "What the hell does this have to do with police work?" Or they would say, "Hey, that's a religion. It's protected by the First Amendment, and there's not a damn thing you can do about it." Our answer would always be the same. We'd tell them that we don't want to do anything about it as a religion, but it seems that when it's there, all these other things are happening. Who's going to tell Mom why her kid killed himself? We're the officers out there. We have to come up with the reasons why he killed himself or why he killed someone else.

You just can't have someone who doesn't know anything about the subject just tell a parent without explanation, "Yeah, your kid was into Satanism, and that's why you're finding all these bones in his closet. He's been sacrificing animals." You just can't lay this on them and leave.

DET. CLEO WILSON: The reaction of our colleagues was all right until we started to build a collection of books and paraphernalia. Then they started to rib us. They would call us "Ghostbusters." That was okay; we could handle it, but it does wear you down sometimes. It takes some of the energy and enthusiasm out of you.

Although our immediate supervisor was encouraging, our lieutenant was not. He said you have to let things go. That makes you feel that what you're doing isn't important. It seems that every time we made the decision to say, the heck with it, we're not going to investigate occult crimes, all of these reports would start coming in. We'd get letters and calls from police asking us what do we know about such and such, and we'd get back into it.

I think our superiors think we're prima donnas because we get calls from other agencies for consultation, and we get requests to give seminars. One thing I've always noticed is that people who have knowledge intimidate those who don't. Instead of learning about it, they become intimidated by it. It's really kind of sad, I think.

DET. BILL WICKERSHAM: Cleo and I got the religious aspect over with at the beginning. We decided that you have to set aside your religious beliefs when you investigate occult crimes. Your badge overrides your religious beliefs. Unfortunately, there are many religious officers out there who see Satanism everywhere, under every rock and behind every tree. This hurts us because they cry wolf a lot. Some crimes are Satanic. There's no doubt about that, but others just seem like it. You have to know the difference and you have to understand the difference. Cleo and I have had clergy ask us to cite Bible scripture when we're handling kids during an alleged occult case. Can you believe it? We will not and cannot do that.

[Det. Mike Barnett is an alias of a detective working for a Northern California county. His agency will not allow him to discuss occult crime publicly.]

DET. MIKE BARNETT: There are police officers out there who are looking at this subject because it interests them from a religious point of view. Many are born-again Christians who believe it's their mission in life to stamp out Satanism and anything else that they believe is anti-Christian. They are on a religious crusade. There's no room in police work for that kind of attitude. You have to be very careful that you don't become linked with one of those guys because you'll be classified as a crusader too. You will lose credibility within your own department because of these guys.

DET. PAT METOYER: One of the problems we have is that one of our Christian officers [in LAPD] tells his wife about some of our cases and before too long she gets interested. We have to have a separation of church and state, and that must be maintained. If there are problems in the law enforcement community with people sacrificing animals [for religious reasons], okay, I can understand that, but if you, as a law enforcement officer, go to the first church and tell them we have a problem, and if they use that to help bolster their congregation that's another problem. Now what happens to me is that instead of having one kook on my hands I have two.

DET. CLEO WILSON: Some of the flak we were getting from our department was because they didn't believe this stuff was happening. We were always trying to justify that it was really going on. We really had to tell them that it wasn't just us, that it wasn't just our area. Occult incidents were happening all over the country. That's why we called people like Sandi Gallant, to exchange information and sometimes just to say, are we crazy? It sounds funny to say this, but we would actually tell our supervisors that we weren't crazy. These things were really happening.

[Det. Greg Bennett is a pseudonym of a detective with the Los Angeles Sheriff's Office. He is currently working undercover and can't have his name made public.]

DET. GREG BENNETT: If the department [Los Angeles Sheriff] found out I was talking to you, I would be fired. We've got strict orders not to talk about this topic. The reason? For one thing, we've got people in the upper echelon of the Sheriff's Department who are members of cults themselves, groups like Scientology, Rosicrucians, the Masons. They say to themselves, If my people are looking at these other cults, how long will it be before they start looking at mine?

Second, the various municipalities don't want it known that this sort of activity takes place. It's embarrassing when the TV folks start taking pictures of occult sites in woods near affluent neighborhoods. It's bad publicity.

The last reason, the one I think is most important, is that the higher-ups have trouble understanding this area. It's nothing they learned when they were in the academy. They feel left out, and as a result they don't want their people doing something they don't understand. Call it jealousy if you want. It's human nature, but it hurts the officers who are trying to do their jobs.

DET. SANDI GALLANT: I've been fortunate compared to some other police officers I speak to. It's taken me years to build up my credibility within my department as someone who doesn't go off half-cocked. They know that if I say something, it's not off the top of my head. I've got documentation.

I'm also very careful to keep the boss informed all the time about what I do. So many cops keep their work to themselves. Politically, that's a mistake. Also, the most important thing is that my boss knows that one belief is always on the top of my mind: I don't investigate religions, I investigate crimes.

You have to learn, learn, learn. You never stop learning. You have to study the ideology of these religions, but you're sitting on that narrow fence because you are studying religion and the First Amendment protects that religion. What isn't protected is the practice if it doesn't fall within the confines of the laws of this country. It's a dilemma that we, as police officers, struggle with all the time.

LETTER TO AUTHOR

CITY OF CHICAGO, POLICE DEPARTMENT

June 24, 1987

Dear Mr. Kahaner:

Your letter of June 16, 1987, to Superintendent Fred Rice, requesting permission to interview Detective Jerry Simandl relative to "non-traditional cults" was referred to me for response.

The Chicago Police Department will not grant permission for Detective Simandl to participate in an interview as a representative of the Chicago Police Department in regards to the subject of cult activities. This topical area has come into the public notice recently and is subject to scrutiny in light of the First Amendment of the United States Constitution. Accordingly, any and all interests expressed by an "official" representative are subject to interpretation of a personal and usually subjective manner.

It is not the intention of the Chicago Police Department to impede appropriate dissemination of this or any other issue to the public. It is important, however, that a public agency not be misinterpreted or otherwise be construed as setting policy or establishing a "theme" with respect to this subject.

> Sincerely,
> John Jemilo
> First Deputy Superintendent
> Bureau of Operational Services

[Darlyne Pettinicchio works for the Orange County, California Probation Department and specializes in juvenile cases. She is also co-founder of The Back In Control Training Center, a private group that helps families in crisis. Many of the youths she deals with are involved in the occult.]

DEPUTY PROBATION OFFICER DARLYNE PETTINICCHIO: There was a kid in Riverside who killed a lady in a school yard. There was a picture of him in the newspaper, and he looked like the All-American boy. What happened to him? If you read the second to the last paragraph it says that the boy dabbled between Catholicism and Satanism. Kids will tell cops, Satan told me to kill my dad, because I knew that if I prayed to God he wouldn't have let me do that. Obviously, there's something there, and a few law enforcement agencies are starting to look at it. Many aren't. I can tell you why they don't want to look at it and why they're hesitant to even say that it's around.

One, it's a religion and it's protected by the law. They

don't want to be held in any lawsuits. People are lawsuit happy, especially here in Southern California.

Second, it's not an area that police know. If you know law enforcement people, you know that they like things they're competent in. They won't tackle stuff they're not. They're very competent in drugs, thefts, burglaries, rapes, and all those kinds of things. They can do a perfect murder investigation. But when they have to start dealing with upside-down crosses on bodies and tongues cut out, they say, Oh, it's just some bizarre, crazy guy. They don't want to admit that it may be part of an organized religious group. It's not in their world.

The agencies that are dealing with it are not saying We're dealing with Satanism, they say, We're dealing with Satanic crime. That takes care of the religious concerns. I've run into cops who tell me that their chief doesn't even want them mentioning the word *Satanism*. I get a lot of that.

There's one more reason. Many of the counties in California are so into PR. How they appear to the public is very important. They don't want to admit that this sort of crime is occurring in their area. The pressure on some police to call crimes anything but Satanic is strong.

DET. PAT METOYER: You have to realize that there are no statutes that cover Witchcraft or Satanism. There are things that occur that have a basis in Satanism, but there is no way that we can collectively put them into a container and say, Okay, we've had this number of Satanic crimes. We can't do that. That's the problem with law enforcement agencies today. There's no way you can justify monitoring a criminal community when you can't show quantitatively that the crime exists. Crimes that appear to have some religious motivation or some deviant activity do not get the kind of reporting or recognition they deserve.

If you're asking whether we need that type of category, however, my answer is no. We can do our jobs, get our convictions without it. In fact, I tell anyone who asks me, don't get into the Satanic stuff with your case. Why? It will give your man an opportunity to plead diminished capacity. Juries have trouble believing this bizarre material. Don't make life difficult for yourself.

If we had a purely Satanic crime in Los Angeles proper, one where the alleged murderer said, "Yeah, I killed him because it was the only ritual I knew that I could perform effectively," if we had one like that, I would say, yes, we had one. We have not.

Let me give you an example: We had one man in L.A. who killed winos. He drank their blood. We had people say, "He's a damn cannibal." Was this boy right in the head? Probably not. So if we, the Police Department, said we had a killer who drank blood, what do you think the news media would do with that? "Vampire Runs Rampant In Los Angeles!" What do you think that does for him when it comes time for his defense? If we called him a cannibal we would build him a defense, because no one in our society is a cannibal. They don't exist to most people. It's the same with Satanism. We're better off not labeling someone a Satanist. If he kills someone, let's call him a killer.

Also, there's the religious aspect. We have two juvenile officers who started looking into gangs and found a phenomenon that no one had paid much attention to. They found one group, the Stoners, that had the ability to move from one area to another with total immunity. That's unheard of in gangs. They were trying to figure out what was going on, and they found that the Stoners were a subculture within the subculture of gangs. They wrote a paper that said the Stoners were similar to a religion. The paper inferred that these people practiced some kind of religious rites.

It was eighty-sixed. The lieutenant who read it said the Los Angeles Police Department is not going to be involved in the suppression of any religious groups. They were asked to recover every copy they gave out. Unfortunately for them, they didn't get them all back.

CHAPTER FOUR:

THE ROOTS OF SATANISM

Like all religions, Satanism borrows beliefs from religions that came before it. Although the first humans may have prayed to spirits or gods whom they considered sometimes good and sometimes evil, the organized act of worshiping an entirely evil entity known as Satan or the Devil didn't appear until the establishment of the Christian church.

In the nineteenth century, such worship coincided with an upsurge in new spiritualism in Europe, a revival of mysticism and ancient Witchcraft and the result was modern day Satanism.

JIM MCCARTHY: Mankind's earliest religion is something called Paganism going back to the upper-ice-age era. That was a time when man was going from hunting and gathering to farming. It was at that time that he acknowledged the need for "technology," which had a lot to do with the survival of the tribe. It's thought that the teachings of this technology, or magick, fell into the hands of a small number of people in that tribe. [Magick spelled with a "k" means the art of producing a desired effect through the use of incantations and other arcane techniques as opposed to magic spelled without a "k," which is what sleight-of-hand artists like The Great Houdini performed.] These people became the shamans or magickians. Often they were special kinds of people like those born blind, with a deformity or with seizures. These people were often considered blessed by the gods. Within the tribes themselves, the secrets of technology were handed down in an oral tradition from parent to child.

This is a natural religion as compared to a revealed religion like Christianity or Judaism. These are called revealed, because the adherents believe that God actually revealed himself to select people. Natural religion grew out of man's need to understand and in some way control nature, like the rain, so his crops would grow. In order to identify and control that facet of nature you had to give it a name and a personality. This is called anthropomorphism. These people identified the forces of nature that played a role in the survival and enrichment of the tribe.

[Jeffrey B. Russell, Ph.D., is a specialist in medieval history. He is a professor of history at the University of California at Santa Barbara. He is the author of several books, former dean of graduate studies at California State University in Sacramento and a Guggenheim Fellow.]

DR. JEFFREY RUSSELL: It's not quite clear that people always thought they were asking for things. Quite frequently we find people in primitive cultures trying to force the gods into giving them things by magick. There are two things here; one is asking, the other is working some magickal spell that will get you the result you want.

Sacrifice, human or animal, can fit into each of these models. It can be a type of magick or part of a prayer. It's hard to say which one it fits under.

Magick is as old as humanity. Magick is simply a manner of technology. It's a way of getting the crops to grow and providing for enough game to last through the season. It's a way of getting people well—or sick, if you don't like them. It's natural that you'll use magick to do the things that you want, especially if you don't have what we today would call advanced technology.

JIM McCARTHY: This natural religion was satisfactory for the needs of many people, but came in conflict with the revealed religions like Christianity and Judaism in the second and third centuries.

As Christianity spread throughout Europe, it was greatly affected by these natural religions. You can see the similarities in the calendars. The Yule season, Easter time, and All Hallow's Eve or Halloween [the eve of All Saint's Day to Christians] were all pagan holidays that Christianity absorbed.

DR. JEFFREY RUSSELL: The term *Paganism* is a catchall word invented primarily by Christians, but to some extent by Jews, in the Roman Empire to designate people who were neither Christians nor Jews. Pagan literally means someone who lives in the countryside, a hick.

What you had was a development of local cults each with their own gods. When a political organization brought these towns into unity, during a conquest for instance, you had the merging of gods. That's how you got the evolution of the major deities in Greek and Roman religions.

Horned gods are found in a lot of religions. It's a symbol of fertility and power. It's not clear why, when the Christians started the process of considering other religions to be demonic, they chose someone with horns as the symbol. It may have something to do with fertility or the sexual connotation of horns. Pan, the horned god in Greco-Roman religions, was associated with wildness, sexual license. That's probably why the Christians incorporated that into their imagery of the devil.

In the early Old Testament there is some entity known as Satan, literally the "adversary," and what you see in Judaism is that entity's personalization. You see that in the Book of Job when this entity argues with God about the treatment of Job. In the first two centuries B.C. you see a very strong tendency in late pre-Christian Judaism to make Satan an important figure.

In the apocalyptic period of Judaism, which starts around 100 B.C. and goes to around A.D. 70 with the fall of the Temple, Satan becomes very strong in Jewish thought. After the fall of the Temple you have the sect of the Pharisees. They believed that the Temple was the center of worship. They were very moral and ethical, and are the founders of rabbinic and Talmudic traditions, which dominate modern Judaism. They downplayed the concept of Satan. So what you had in Judaism was a very strong emphasis on Satan for a couple of hundred years then ended with the triumph of the Pharisees.

With Christianity, which begins with apocalyptic Judaism, you see an interest in Satan that becomes part of their core doctrine.

[James Le Bar is a priest and consultant on the occult to the Archdiocese of New York. In 1976, Cardinal Cooke's office asked him to look into cults following the growth of cult groups such as the Unification Church. His interest in the occult grew from that work. He is a member of the Interfaith Coalition of New York City.]

FATHER JAMES LE BAR: To be a practicing Catholic one must necessarily believe in the Devil. In Catholic theology, we teach that God created all things, and before he created man he created higher creatures called angels. In the due course of time, just as he gives man a test of his faithfulness, he gave angels a test to prove theirs. The angels, having a higher intelligence, had only one chance. Those who did not pass the test, those who disobeyed God, became the fallen angels, the leader of which is Satan or the Devil. That's part of Catholic theology. Many people push it to the background or prefer not to bring it forth consciously, but it is part of Catholic teaching.

In the New Testament, Jesus refers to Beelzebub as the prince of devils and Lucifer as the light bearer. Over the centuries, we've referred to them all as the Devil. Satan is considered the leader of devils. It's hard to distinguish them from each other. They all pretty much refer to the same creature.

DR. JEFFREY RUSSELL: A group known as the Gnostics came out of the first century B.C. and were closely tied to Judaism and Christianity. Scholars debate whether they were a heresy or an independent religion.

The Gnostics had a dualistic view of the world; good versus evil, matter versus spirit. This god of matter they looked at as being evil with enormous power. He was the ruler of matter, which they deemed evil. Sometimes they called it the Devil, sometimes they didn't. What's important is that they elevated an evil spirit, which grew out of Judaism and Christianity, to an enormous level of power.

Two things happened. Christians rejected and condemned it, but at the same time they were subtly influenced by it. There was a carry over from Gnosticism to Christianity, especially the importance of this evil god which reinforces the belief in the Christian Devil. There was a mini boom in the Devil during that time.

[Carl A. Raschke, Ph.D., specializes in philosophy and religious studies. He is a professor of religion at the University of Denver's Department of Religion. He is the author of several books, including one about Gnosticism.]

DR. CARL RASCHKE: There was a group called the Bogomils. They came out of Southeast Europe, mainly Bulgaria. Bulgaria has always been a hotbed of heresy. One reason is that it was the center of agricultural goddess worship and fertility worship going back to the Stone Age.

The Bogomil heresy became the basis of Cathari belief. The Cathars were a fairly powerful, perfectionist group. What both groups believed was that this world had been created by

Lucifer, and Jesus had not redeemed this world, and because they lived on this world they had to worship Satan. They believed that God and Satan were equal.

[The Cathars were considered heretics by the Church because of their belief that God was not all-powerful. In 1208, Pope Innocent III declared a crusade against them which lasted twenty years. After that time, the Cathars carried on an underground war against the Inquisition that had been started by Pope Gregory IX. The Cathars were all but crushed in 1244 when two hundred were killed during battles.]

[Duane J. Osheim, Ph.D. is an expert in Medieval and Renaissance history. He is a professor of history at the University of Virginia in Charlottesville.]

DR. DUANE OSHEIM: The Knights Templar were a group of knightly monks started in the twelveth century under Saint Bernard as a crusading order that would help liberate the Holy Land and the Temple of Jerusalem. It was a popular device in those days to have a crusading order, and the Templars were the most famous. Basically, they were military men invented by the church.

[The Templars took a vow of chastity. They were even forbidden to kiss their mothers. This total avoidance of females led to rumors of homosexuality.

Two major factors distinguished the Templars from other orders: devotion to fighting and secrecy about the internal workings of the order. The Templars also received papal immunity from taxes and exemption from secular laws.]

By the fourteenth century, they still had modest military functions, but they were probably more important as bankers and merchants. They specialized in transferring money from one place to another. This makes them very important in the history of banking and finance.

[Although the Crusades were a failure, the Templars grew powerful and wealthy, and many people resented them. The rich despised their immunity and great power compared to the monarch, and the lower classes resented them because they didn't have to pay taxes on the goods they traded even though everyone else paid taxes on their traded goods.]

By the fourteenth century there were enough rumors about the Templars that the king of France, Philip IV, decided to investigate them. [Historians suggest that Philip wanted to ruin the Templars to get their wealth and cancel his debts to them. At one time he tried to join the order but didn't succeed so he began a campaign against them. During this period, heresy was always an acceptable charge.]

In the process of investigation, after subjecting them to a variety of tortures, the Inquisitors managed to wring confessions out of them that seemed to indicate knowledge of Satanic cults and homosexual acts. How much truth you can put into these confessions is hard to determine. The kinds of confessions they made strike you as the type of things people expected to hear. Everybody sort of knew what the myths were so when they put you on the rack and started bending your fingers around, you're more than willing to tell them what they want to hear.

[It was charged that the Templars prayed to a Baphomet, which was described as a stuffed human head or goat head, and also worshiped the Devil in the form of a black cat. The Baphomet as a goat head is seen in modern Satanic rituals and is sometimes considered the symbol of that belief.]

Whether the Templars engaged in Satanism or anything else heretic almost doesn't matter because the myths became fixed in the fifteenth century by a group of Dominicans, the people who wrote the *Malleus Maleficarum*. [This book, written in 1486, was a handbook for witch hunters describing in great detail how to spot witches and prosecute them. There were sixteen German editions, eleven French, two Italian and later an English.

Some of the charges against the Templars may have been true. In such a closed, male, and secret society homosexuality is not uncommon, and in order to maintain *esprit de corps* and bolster their image as a powerful union, some members may have practiced ritual magick learned on their treks to the Orient.]

One thing that comes across is that the authorities, in stamping out these alleged heresies, sort of forced people into perceptions of what the demons, rituals, and so forth are supposed to be.

DR. DUANE OSHEIM: The Black Mass is an inversion of the Christian Mass, and initially it was not Satanic. You can trace the Black Mass back to the invention of the Antichrist around the eighth century. There was no mention of an Antichrist in the Bible, but once you invent it, it sets up a host of activities like the Black Mass. Once it gets codified by Catholic writers, you have a body of knowledge, and it doesn't even matter if it was true or not. Also, you have people practicing it, because they were told about it by the church.

[Nobody knows the origin of the Black Mass or when it was first practiced. It is however related to a Catholic Mass in that a church Mass is supposed to bring to the congregation an all-powerful holy spirit as a force for healing, peace, and good. It's thought that priests, perhaps swelled with the power and spirit they conjured in the name of God, saw the Black Mass as a way to do their carnal bidding as well.

The first Black Mass to be cited was at the seventh century Church Council of Toledo in which the church denounced the Mass of the Dead. In this rite, the priest didn't deliver the soul of a dead man from purgatory but consigned a living man to death.

The Mass of Saint Secaraire originated in Gascony was

supposed to have been performed in an abandoned or ramshackle church. The priest's server is a woman with whom he has had intercourse. The Mass is similar to a Catholic Mass, but the priest consecrates a black triangular host and instead of wine uses water from a well in which an unbaptized baby has drowned. The end result is the death of an intended victim.]

FATHER JAMES LE BAR: For the most part, the Black Mass is a perversion of the Catholic Mass. Certain Satanic worship comprises the exact opposite of what the Catholic church does. So the Black Mass actually was not the original type of Satan worship, but it developed in the Middle Ages and later and those priests who were no longer faithful to their calling began this form of hatred of the church which turns into Devil worship. Today, like so many other areas, this is regarded as a primary method of Satan worship, but it's not the original nor is it the only one.

DR. JEFFREY RUSSELL: The Black Mass was popular during the reign of King Louis XIV in the seventeenth century.

[During the seventeenth century, a woman named Catherine Deshayes, also known as Madame LaVoison, used a Black Mass and its magick to cast spells on people, especially to win back wayward lovers for well-to-do clients. She also used her activities as a way of distributing love potions and poisons to ladies of high social status. She also did astrology, performed abortions, and supplied adults with children for the purpose of sexual abuse.

During these masses, the blood of sacrificed babies was used instead of wine and their flesh took the role of host. Ordained priests officiated at the masses, often saying the Catholic Mass backwards, turning crucifixes upside down and using black candles instead of white. The candles were made from human fat supplied by a public executioner. A furnace was found in LaVoison's house, which she said was used to dispose of sacrificed babies and aborted fetuses.

LaVoison's arrest was the result of a special court established by Louis XIV in 1679 to deal with numerous poisonings of French nobility. It also may have been in response to a flood of unexplained disappearances of children which prompted public riots in 1676. The police officer in charge was Nicholas de la Reymie, the police commissioner of Paris. His investigations went from poison to magick and, like his modern counterparts, he took a great deal of ridicule about his accusations of occult activity. He finally stopped his investigations when the King's mistress, Madame de Montespan, became implicated.

LaVoison was burned at the stake in 1680 after a lengthy investigation. Some of her activities were similar to those described in current-day ritualized abuse cases of children discussed in Chapter 12.]

DR. JEFFREY RUSSELL: The Black Mass seems to disappear until the nineteenth century when you see some cults in France reviving it. Then you find the Black Mass popping in and out of the occult tradition.

DR. CARL RASCHKE: Public Satanism, people who proclaim themselves to practice Satanism, is really a twentieth century phenomenon. It has to do with the decline of the power and influence of the Catholic church. Nobody could call themselves Satanists or openly practice it as late as the eighteenth century without immediate persecution, torture, or burning.

The beginnings of what we might call modern Satanism can be traced to the late romantic era of the nineteenth century, the so-called occult revival in countries like France and England.

Crowley's movement, for instance, comes out of the Order

of the Golden Dawn. The Golden Dawn comes out of various renegade versions of Scottish Rites and Masonry, what I call "genteel occultism." They are very eclectic and very confusing.

[In the early 1880s, an ex-Catholic seminarian named Alphonse Louis Constant rediscovered the Kabbalah, a magickal school of thought that was developed in Babylon in the early Middle Ages and stems from ancient Hebrew sources. The Kabbalists believed the world could be grasped through the manipulation of numbers and letters. The number 10 is the organizing principle of the universe, and each of ten steps or "sephirot" on a "tree" takes the practitioner closer to the divine. He climbs the trees using knowledge and magick. Each sephirot stands for an aspect of God: being or existence, wisdom, intelligence or understanding, mercy or love, strength, beauty, firmness, glory, foundation, and kingdom.

The Tarot was also developed during this time. Each of the seventy-eight cards carries an occult symbol, much of it related to the Kabbalah.

Constant took an occult pen name, Eliphas Levi, and his writings influenced a whole new generation of magickal practitioners and spiritualists, many of whom established their own groups. One was the Order of the Golden Dawn, whose adherents believed in an Hermetic principle of correspondence between the human being and the universe. Any principle that exists in the universe exists in man, and a trained occultist can become attuned to these cosmic forces. He can call forces from outside the body or from within his own self. The method used to accomplish this is called ritual magick.

This notion of correspondence between the person and the universe and the idea that power exists in both places waiting to be summoned is the basis for New Age religions popular today.

As in most magickal groups, including the Freemasons, the Order of the Golden Dawn had steps or degrees to climb based on a practitioner's ability. The most famous member of the Order of the Golden Dawn was Aleister Crowley. Crowley moved up quickly in the order but was refused a high tier because of his moral perversions which included homosexual acts with minors, cocaine and ether addictions, and allegedly murder.

Crowley practiced and codified sex magick, a body of spiritualism that believes in the emission of energy during sexual climax that can be harnessed and used for rituals. He placed ads in newspapers for deformed people with whom he would have sex. He believed that the more deformed a person, the more sexual energy they would unleash.

Crowley considered himself the "Beast" and called himself "666" after the Bible's passage in Revelation: "You shall know the Beast, for he is a man, and his number is 666." Bible students disagree, but many believe the number 666 was a numerical equivalent of the name Neron Caesar, spelled more commonly without the second *n*. Neron Caesar was hated by those under his rule.

Crowley's writings stessed the theme: "Do what thou wilt, shall be the whole of the Law," the opposite of the Bible's golden rule. Because of his actions, Crowley found himself deported from many different countries throughout his life.

Around the turn of the century, a German named Karl Keller founded the *Ordo Templi Orientis* or OTO, which practiced perverse sex magick, and Crowley became the head of its British chapter.

Ritual magick came to North America from Britain through members of the Order of the Golden Dawn during the early 1900s. Before World War I, the OTO had opened chapters in Vancouver, B.C., Los Angeles, and Washington, D.C. The current OTO chapters in North America dispute direct lineage to the original OTO.]

DR. CARL RASCHKE: Anything I say about the origins of modern Satanic cults is speculative because one is dealing with secret societies and secret traditions and conspiratorial groups who deliberately don't leave documentary traces. In many cases, they obfuscated what they were up to in order to mislead the authorities or their potential enemies.

Modern Satanism begins with the effort to try to define occultism in an honest way, an extreme way and in a theatrical way. What Crowley was doing with Satanism in England in the 1920s and 1930s, is somewhat like what Anton LaVey was doing in the 1960s in San Francisco. It was a way of shocking the bourgeois and also promoting himself as a kind of celebrity. If you read Crowley's writing there's a lot of black magick but there's a good deal of Hermeticism, Gnosticism and so forth. It's safe to say that real hardcore Satanism is a variation of this self-glorifying and brutal outlook. It's a variation of traditional occultism.

Satanism always flourished during times of cultural decadence, when decadence is in fashion, when you have a particular ruling class in a country that feels threatened or is being besieged by new economic classes to where they're losing their prestige and political authority. The period between the world wars in England was a time of social experimentation, a period of nihilism. The ruling class in England had lost its taste for rule; it was a period of outraged scandal and decadence. Occultists like Crowley flourished in that time.

DR. JEFFREY RUSSELL: My view of modern Satanism, as a religious movement, is that it's pretty incoherent, although it has had a great effect on people of unsound mind. Some people have been psychologically damaged by it. There's no doubt about that.

Modern Satanism does have ties to the occult movements of the nineteenth century, Black Mass, and Crowley. Another origin, I believe, is with the popular culture of horror and with the counterculture movement of the 1960s.

CHAPTER FIVE:

THE THREE FACES
OF SATAN

*S*ome investigators have divided Satanism into different groups, each having its own characteristics. This division makes it easier to understand the participants' actions and motivations. Not everyone agrees on the exact delineations, however. In fact, some people reject the notion of clear-cut differences altogether, because the practice of Satanism is often subject to the whim and caprice of its individual followers.

The groups named in this chapter, The Church of Satan, Temple of Set, etc., are bona fide religious groups. Their beliefs are protected by law, and there is no evidence linking these groups with illegal activity. Law enforcement officials do worry, however, about certain individuals or groups within these groups who take the groups' ideas and pervert them.

DET. SANDI GALLANT: There are three kinds of Satanic groups. The first group I label traditional or orthodox. I find them to be highly organized, and they have a spiritual base. They have set up their group to worship Satan in some particular form. The form is usually devised by the group itself, and it may differ from group to group. Some may be open and public. Others may be closed and private. They may look upon Satan in different ways, too. Some may refer to him as Satan. Others, like The Temple of Set, may refer to him as Set, the ancient Egyptian god of the dead.

These groups are very structured, and they may contain degrees of order within that structure. For instance, those at the bottom of the totem pole are made to feel that. You'll also find generational linkages in some organized groups, passed on as religion from generation to generation just like any other religion.

In this group I would put the Church of Satan, the Temple of Set and the Process Church of the Final Judgement. [Other orthodox groups include: Our Lady of Endor Coven, the Ophite Cultus Satanis, founded in 1948 by Herbert Sloane in Toledo, Ohio; Brotherhood of the Ram, a southern California group; Church of Satanic Brotherhood, which broke away from the Church of Satan in the early 1970s over disagreements with Anton LaVey, and Thee Satanic Orthodox Church of Nethilum Rite, located in Chicago, which was formed in 1971.]

There are other orthodox Satanic groups that exist whose names we'll never know, because they are not made public. These, in fact, may be the most dangerous of all. [Groups usually go public by incorporation, enjoying the tax-exempt status of traditional religions, or by owning or affiliating themselves with bookstores from which they sell their books and paraphernalia.]

It's also important to note that those in orthodox groups outside of the Church of Satan may not look upon the Church of Satan as an orthodox group anymore. They think that the church is just a gathering organization that brings in nothing more than groupies. You can join by mail by filling out a questionnaire and paying your money [$100].

As far as crime is concerned, I don't worry about Anton LaVey's Church of Satan group in San Francisco. I can't make any statements for them outside of San Francisco. LaVey would have to be a raving lunatic to do anything illegal. He's very high profile. However, there are people who attach themselves to his group, scattered throughout the country, who may be involved in criminal conduct. On the whole, I don't worry that much about any organized high profile group.

[Anton LaVey, the high priest of the Church of Satan, didn't respond to the author's request for an interview. The following material is from those familiar with LaVey and the Church's activities.

Anton LaVey was born in Chicago on April 11, 1930. His father was a liquor salesman; the family later moved to San Francisco. When LaVey was a teenager, he developed an interest in the occult. At seventeen he joined the Clyde Beatty Circus as a cage boy, then as an assistant lion trainer. He also played the calliope for Hugo Zachinni, the human cannonball, and the Flying Wallendas.

At eighteen he left the circus and joined a carnival. According to LaVey's biographer, Burton H. Wolfe, who wrote *The Devil's Avenger: A Biography of Anton Szandor LaVey* in 1974, what he saw at the carnival made an impression on LaVey. "On Saturday night," Wolfe quotes LaVey as saying, "I would see men lusting after half-naked girls dancing at the carnival and on Sunday morning when I was playing organ for tent show evangelists at the other end of the carnival lot, I would see these same men sitting in the pews with their wives and children asking God to forgive them and purge them of carnal desires. And the next Saturday night they'd be back at the carnival or some other place of indulgence. I knew then that the Christian Church thrives on hypocrisy and that man's carnal nature will out no matter how much is purged or scourged by any white light religion."

Apparently, this was the germ of LaVey's idea for the Church of Satan, a body that would praise indulgence as opposed to preaching abstinence.

In 1951, LaVey, now married, left the carnival and enrolled in the City College of San Francisco. He took a job as a photographer for the San Francisco Police Department and stayed there for three years. Seeing the seamy, violent side of life through his work, LaVey again questioned the concept of a Christian god. He was bothered by people's self-righteous attitude about violence, saying it was God's will. After leaving the Police Department LaVey began playing the organ in nightclubs, and he began dabbling in the Black Arts. He bought a house in San Francisco's Richmond district; the building was to become the site of Black Arts parties and gatherings.

In 1960, LaVey divorced his first wife and married his second wife, Diane, to whom *The Satanic Bible*, published in 1969, was dedicated. For the next several years, LaVey began holding seminars, lectures and meetings about the Black Arts at his house. He eventually attracted a steady group known as the Magic Circle.

On April 30, 1966, the occult holiday of Walpurgis-nacht, LaVey shaved his head, put on a clerical collar, neatly trimmed his Mephistophelian beard and proclaimed the age of Satan. LaVey encouraged coverage by the news media which viewed his newly formed Church of Satan as an oddity or carnival curiosity.

He was being called The Black Pope. He engaged in Black Masses in which a member would dress like the Pope. During the ceremony a nude woman was used as an altar as the make-believe Pope engaged in apparent sexual intercourse for the sake of the cameras.

LaVey continued to grab the headlines. In May 1967, he baptized his daughter Zeena into the Church of Satan. The baptism was recorded and the record was released the following year. Later on, LaVey was invited to act as a consultant on the set of *Rosemary's Baby*, the hit movie about a group of Satanists who use the wife (Mia Farrow) of an aspiring actor (John Cassavetes) to breed the devil's child. LaVey is listed in the credits as an advisor.

The Church of Satan continued to attract attention. A U.S. Navy Seaman, who had been a member of the Church, died, and LaVey, accompanied by filmmaker and friend Kenneth Anger, officiated at the funeral along with a Navy Honor Guard. The Church had gained legitimacy, so much so that the U.S. Government eventually provided its chaplains with a handbook that, along with other non-traditional religions, describes the religious needs of service people who belong to the Church of Satan. The information came from the Church itself.]

RELIGIOUS REQUIREMENTS AND PRACTICES OF CERTAIN SELECTED GROUPS
A HANDBOOK FOR CHAPLAINS

The work involved in developing and producing this handbook was performed pursuant to contract number MDA903 76 C 0267 with the U.S. Department of Defense by:
    Kirchner Associates, Inc.
    with subcontract work by:
    The Institute for the Study of American Religion

CHURCH OF SATAN   ANTON S. LAVEY
Post Office Box 7633
San Francisco, CA 94120
High Priest   AKA: Satanists

HISTORICAL ROOTS: The Church of Satan is an eclectic body that traces its origins to many sources— classical voodoo, the Hell Fire club of 18th century

England, the ritual magic of Aleister Crowley and the Black Order of Germany in the 1920s and 1930s.

CURRENT WORLD LEADER: Anton Szandor LaVey, High Priest.

NUMBER OF ADHERENTS IN THE U.S.: Between 10,000 and 20,000.

ORGANIZATIONAL STRUCTURE: The Church of Satan is focused in the Central Grotto in San Francisco. It accepts or rejects all potential members and charters other grottos around the country. Isolated individuals relate directly to the Central Grotto.

LEADERSHIP AND ROLE OF PRIESTS: The Priesthood is not comprised of individuals who are necessarily adept in the performance of rituals, though pastoral and organizational abilities are not minimized. The rank of Priest is conferred on those who have achieved a measurable degree of esteem or success; one's level of membership within the church is commensurate with his/her position outside the church. Hence, a respected career soldier or commissioned officer in the Army might qualify, though be totally uninvolved with group activity. Rituals are conducted by a *de facto* priest, i.e., a celebrant member who has evidenced a working knowledge of and ability to conduct services and is authorized by the central Grotto.

WHO MAY CONDUCT A RITUAL? Anyone, but a priest is required for group worship.

IS GROUP WORSHIP REQUIRED? No, but it is strongly encouraged, because it is a strong reinforcement of the faith and instillation of power.

WORSHIP REQUIREMENTS: Worship in the Church of Satan is based upon the belief that man needs ritual, dogma, fantasy and enchantment. Worship consists of magickal rituals and there are three basic kinds: sexual rituals to fulfill a desire; compassionate rituals, to help another; and destructive rituals, used for anger, annoyance or hate. Grottos often gather on Friday evenings for group rituals.

MINIMUM EQUIPMENT FOR WORSHIP: Varies with the type of ritual performed but is likely to include a black robe, an altar, the symbol of Baphomet, candles, bell, a chalice, elixir (wine or some other drink most pleasing to the palate), sword, model phallus, gong, and parchment.

FACILITIES FOR WORSHIP: A private place where an altar can be erected and rituals performed.

SPECIAL RELIGIOUS HOLIDAYS: The highest holiday is one's own birthday. Every man is a God if he chooses to recognize that fact. After one's birthday, Walpurgisnacht (April 30) and Halloween are most important. April 30 is the grand climax of the spring equinox and Halloween was one of the times of the great fire festivals among the ancient Druids. The solstices and equinoxes—which fall in March, June, September and December and mark the first day of the new seasons—are also celebrated.

FUNERAL AND BURIAL REQUIREMENTS: The priests of the Church of Satan perform funerals and the Central Grotto should be contacted in case of death.

AUTOPSY: No restrictions.

CREMATIONS: Only permitted in extreme circumstances such as an expedient measure where it is necessary to safeguard the health of others.

MEDICAL TREATMENT: No restrictions.

UNIFORM APPEARANCE REQUIREMENTS: No restrictions.

POSITION ON SERVICE IN THE ARMED FORCES: None.

ANY OTHER PRACTICES OR TEACHINGS WHICH MAY CONFLICT WITH MILITARY DIRECTIVES OR PRACTICES: None.

BASIC TEACHINGS OR BELIEFS: The Church of Satan worships Satan, most clearly symbolized in the Roman God Lucifer, the bearer of light, the spirit of the air, and the personification of enlightenment. Satan is not visualized as an anthropomorphic being, rather he represents the forces of nature. To the Satanist, the self is the highest embodiment of human life and is sacred. The Church of Satan is essentially a human potential movement and members are encouraged to develop whatever capabilities they can by which they might excel. They are, however, cautioned to recognize their limitations—an important factor in this philosophy of rational self-interest. Satanists practice magick, the art of changing situations or events in accordance with one's will, which would, using normally accepted methods, be impossible.

CREEDAL STATEMENTS AND AUTHORITATIVE LITERATURE: The writings of Anton LaVey provide the direction for the Satanists—*The Satanic Bible, The Compleat Witch* and *The Satanic Rituals*. Members are encouraged to study pertinent writings which serve as guidelines for the Satanic thought such as works of Mark Twain, Niccolo Machiavelli, G. S. Shaw, Ayn Rand, Friedrich Nietzsche, etc.

ETHICAL PRACTICES: The ethical stance of the Church of Satan is summarized in the Nine Satanic Statements.

THE NINE SATANIC STATEMENTS

1. Satan represents indulgence instead of abstinence!
2. Satan represents vital existence, instead of spiritual pipe dreams!
3. Satan represents undefiled wisdom, instead of hypocritical self-deceit!
4. Satan represents kindness to those who deserve it, instead of love wasted on ingrates!
5. Satan represents vengeance instead of turning the other cheek!
6. Satan represents responsibility to the responsible, instead of concern for psychic vampires!
7. Satan represents man as just another animal, sometimes better, sometimes worse than those that walk on all-fours, who, because of his "divine spiritual and intellectual development," has become the most vicious animal of all!
8. Satan represents all of the so-called sins, as they all lead to physical, mental or emotional gratification!
9. Satan has been the best friend the church has ever had, as he has kept it in business all these years!

Beyond the above principles, Satanists generally op-
pose the use of narcotics which dull the senses and
suicide which cuts off the life (the great indulgence)
and stand firmly on law and order. The Church of Satan is not to be confused with Satanist groups which
have been found to engage in illegal acts.

**HOW DOES THE CHURCH OF SATAN RECRUIT NEW
MEMBERS?** The Church does not proselytize but wel-
comes inquiries from honest potential Satanists who
hear about the Church from the various books about
it, the mass media or word of mouth.

RELATIONSHIP WITH OTHER RELIGIONS: The
Church of Satan stands as a gathering point for all
those who believe in what the Christian Church opposes, and members are generally hostile to its
teachings and resultant behavior patterns. To a
lesser extent, the same position holds for Eastern religions.

[In 1975, some members of the Church of Satan became
displeased with LaVey and what they perceived as the church's
new direction. They thought the Church to be too high profile,
too media conscious and too much like a circus side show.
They also believed that LaVey's ego was becoming more important than the church's mission. Many senior members quit
and began their own groups. One of these people was Michael
Aquino.

Aquino joined the Church of Satan after serving nine
months in Vietnam as a lieutenant in the cavalry squadron
for the 82nd Airborne. When he flew home to San Francisco
in 1969 to be married, he was looking for a dose of counterculture, something to even out the effects of Army regimen-
tation. He saw an advertisement for the Church of Satan in
the *Berkeley Barb*, an underground newspaper.

Aquino, his fiancée, and a few friends set out for LaVey's house. He later described LaVey as tall, about six feet, and heavily built without being fat. He reminded Aquino of a "grizzly bear on its hind legs." But the man wasn't posturing, Aquino remembers, his manner was relaxed and did not radiate defensiveness. He enjoyed himself and what he was doing. Aquino was intrigued by his confidence.

The two became close over the years and LaVey raised Aquino to the full level of IV°—Magister Templi—the first Satanist other than LaVey to attain this level. The recognition was conveyed on August 5, 1973, the anniversary of Marilyn Monroe's death.

LaVey was fascinated with Monroe and members of the Church claimed that LaVey held a ritual of necromancy for her. LaVey believed that Monroe's death wasn't suicide. Like others, he believed that her death was connected with her alleged relationships with John and Robert Kennedy. The ceremony apparently bolstered that belief.

Aquino believed that the Church was becoming corrupt. For one thing, he believed that it erred in letting outsiders visit, study, and observe the Church without any intention of personal commitment. The Church elders believed that if people were exposed to the Church philosophy they would make such a commitment. Aquino believed that was wrong. He believed that people vampirized the Church, enjoyed the accessories of the philosophy (the indulgence without guilt) and contributed very little. Aquino decided to start his own Satanic cult and vowed not to make the same mistakes as the Church of Satan.

The group was actually an offshoot of an order within the Church of Satan known as The Order of the Trapezoid. As opposed to modern magick with a Mediterranean origin, the Order emphasized magick from Northern Europe and Germany. Germanic mysticism developed mostly on its own and remained isolated during the Roman rule of Europe. It resurfaced during the Second and Third Reichs in Germany, much of it the basis for the Nazis' obsession with the Black Arts. According to some members within the Church of Satan, the Order attempted to reconstruct this German mysticism. According to others, however, it had unpleasant overtones of Nazism.

While still a member of the Church of Satan, Aquino spelled out the tenets of the Temple of Set in *The Book of Coming Forth by Night*. The title is the antithesis of *The Book of Coming Forth by Day*, also known as the Egyptian *Book of the Dead*. Aquino says that *The Book* came to him after he called upon the Prince of Darkness and his coming forth. In it, Set declares the Age of Satan to be over and the Age of Set beginning. Set says that his pact with LaVey is over. "Upon the ninth solstice, I destroyed my pact with Anton Szandor LaVey. . . . Thus all may understand that he (LaVey) is dearly held by me, and that the Church of Satan is not a thing of shame to him. But a new Aeon is now to begin, and the work of Anton Szandor LaVey is done."]

DR. MICHAEL AQUINO: After a series of complex cere-monial procedures and evocations on the night of the North Solstice 1975, I sat down at the desk in my study in Santa Barbara, California, and wrote out *The Book of Coming Forth by Night* in a single sitting, from approximately midnight to 4 A.M., as I recall. It was a deliberate, reflective act rather than a spasmodic or theatrical one. My only feelings were of hyper-intense concentration and a sense of great dignity—coupled with a reverent sense of what I can only describe as authen-ticity. At 4 A.M., I looked at the pages before me and accepted them with my entire being, and the rest is history.

[*The Crystal Tablet of Set* was written by Michael Aquino.]

CRYSTAL TABLET OF SET: While the Temple of Set as an organization was formally incorporated in 1975 C.E., [Satanists prefer to use C.E. meaning Common Era, instead of A.D. for Anno Domini, the Year of Our Lord. In addition, many will reckon time starting with 1966 as year one, when LaVey declared the modern age of Satan] its magical and philosophical roots are prehistoric, originating in mankind's first apprehension that there is "something different" about the human race—a sense of self-consciousness that places humanity apart from and above all other known forms of life.

Ancient religions—of which those of Egypt are generally acknowledged the eldest—either exalted or feared this self-consciousness. Those who exalted it took the position that the human psyche is capable of opposition to a domination of the forces of nature. Those fearing it warned man that such a presumption of independence would be sinful and dangerous. Therefore, they said such "will to power" should be concealed, sublimated—and if necessary punished and exterminated— that mankind might return to an Eden-like state of nature untroubled by the burdens of having to take responsibility for decisions, judgments and actions based upon an essentially personal determination of good and evil.

While all philosophical schools embraced the psychocentric consciousness to some degree, there were very few that made it avowedly and explicitly the focus of their attention. The divine personification (gods) of such schools have come down to us as symbols of what worshipers of non-consciousness consider the supreme evil, the Prince of Darkness in his many forms. Of these, the most ancient is Set, whose priesthood can be traced to predynamic times. Images of Set have been dated to ca 3200 B.C.E. with astronomically based estimates of inscriptions dating to ca 5000 B.C.E.

DR. MICHAEL AQUINO: In ancient Egyptian mythology, Set is represented either as an animal with a long nose, stiffly upraised ears and a forked tail or as a male human body with the head of the aforementioned animal. The Temple of Set uses this image because of its traditional symbolism of the god—or more precisely Neter, in Egyptian hieroglyphics—meaning one of the key principles of the cosmos. We conceptualize Set as a center of intelligence far more abstract. It's what Plato would call the form of the independent self-aware psyche. While we perceive this entity as quite real—as real as your own sense of self-contained being—we don't envision it as an anthropomorphic creature any more than you would represent your own psyche in such a manner.

CRYSTAL TABLET: Conventional religions, with their colorful mythologies analyzed in terms of the underlying philosophical principles, represent simply the primitive longing of mankind to feel "at one" with the universal harmony he perceives about him. White magic as practiced by primitive pagan and modern institutional religions offers devotees the illusion of "reinclusion" in the universal scheme of things through ritualistic devotions and superstitions.

The Black Magickian on the other hand rejects both the desirability of union with the universe and any self-deceptive antics designed to create such an illusion. He has considered the existence of the individual psyche—the real you of the conscious intelligence—and has taken satisfaction from its existence as something unlike anything else in the universe. The Black Magickian desires this psyche to live, to experience, to continue. He does not wish to die or to lose his consciousness and identity to a larger universal consciousness. He wants to be. This decision in favor of individual existence is the first premise of the Temple of Set.

The second premise is that the psychocentric consciousness can evolve towards its own divinity through deliberate exercise of the intelligence and will, a process of becoming or coming into being.

DR. MICHAEL AQUINO: Knowledge and application and exercise of that knowledge are the crucial factors in the Temple of Set. Faith isn't a factor. In fact, we disapprove of any unsupported excuse for knowledge such as this. Accordingly, we don't expect our initiates to take the Temple's philosophy, cosmology and magickal theories as acts of faith but rather to consider them working hypotheses perhaps more meaningful to one person than to another and to develop or not develop confidence in them through personal experimentation and exercise.

CRYSTAL TABLET: Supreme authority in the Temple is held by the Council of Nine, which appoints both the High Priest of Set and the Executive Director. Initiates are recognized according to six degrees based on Western Magickal tradition and incorporating features from many Black Magickal societies: Setian I°, Adept II°, Priest or Priestess of Set III°, Magister/Magistra Templi IV°, Magus/Maga V° and Ipsissimus/Ipsissima VI°. Recognition as an Adept constitutes certification that one has in fact mastered and successfully applied the essential principles of Black Magick.

DR. MICHAEL AQUINO: I am a Lieutenant Colonel in the Army on active duty, working in resource management. I am a graduate of the National Defense University in Washington, D.C. Beyond that, I would rather not discuss the details of my military career as, in the American tradition of separation of church and state, I endeavor not to confuse the two or invoke one in a context pertinent to the other.

I have a Ph.D. in political science from the University of California, Santa Barbara, and a Master of Public Administration from George Washington University in Washington, D.C. I have also taught political science for several years as an adjunct professor at Golden Gate University in San Francisco.

The title of my doctoral dissertation was "The Neutron Bomb." As it was in the field of Political Science, it dealt with the U.S., European, and Soviet negotiations concerning the development and possible deployment of neutron weapons in NATO during the Carter administration. Its principal theme —other than being a historical survey of the episode—was that the perceptions upon which many of the actors based their decisions were not necessarily related to the facts, nor were decisions made with a clear strategic foreign policy necessarily in mind.

Interestingly enough, my research led me to conclude that Jimmy Carter was a careful and methodical decision-maker where the neutron issue was concerned. This is in refutation to his popular image as an indecisive and weak leader.

As a matter of policy, the Temple of Set does not give out membership numbers. [Sources close to the Temple estimate the number at under one hundred.] The bulk of our membership is spread fairly evenly throughout the United States with other members in Europe, Canada, and some Pacific Basin countries. Most of those who contact us wash out before even applying to join. They are discouraged by the rather dry membership informational letter we issue. Of those who apply for I° admission, perhaps half don't attain recognition as Adept II° within the two-year time limit. There is virtually no attrition beyond the II° level, though we have had a few senior initiates who have either resigned for personal reasons or been expelled for abuse of their responsibilities, the last such occurrence being about five years ago.

CRYSTAL TABLET: The Temple of Set enjoys the colorful legacy of the Black Arts and we use many forms of historical Satanic imagery for our stimulation and pleasure. But we have not found that any interest or activity which an enlightened mature intellect would regard as undignified, sadistic, criminal, or depraved is desirable, much less essential, to our work.

The Black Arts are dangerous in the same way that working with volatile chemicals is dangerous. This is most emphatically not a field of unstable, immature, or otherwise emotionally or intellectually weak-minded people. Such are a hazard to themselves and to others with whom they come in contact. The Temple endeavors not to admit them to begin with. If such an individual should gain admittance and later be exposed he will be summarily expelled. In cases of doubt, the Temple may be expected to place the burden of proof on the individual for the sake of all Setians and the Temple's integrity . . . Under no circumstance is any life form ever sacrificed or injured in a Black Magickal Working of the Temple of Set. Violation of this rule will result in the offender's immediate expulsion and referral to law enforcement or animal protection authorities . . . The Temple is a forum for the investigation of many subjects which conventional society finds odd, mysterious, and even extremely frightening. The Temple will be tolerated only to the extent that it is known to be pursuing its interests carefully, expertly, and responsibly. It occupies a delicate position in a world which is largely unhappy with itself and which is ceaselessly searching for scapegoats. Hence the Temple must take care to maintain its social balance with prudence and dignity.

DR. MICHAEL AQUINO: Social abuses which would be, and regularly are, tolerated and excused in conventional religions would be unacceptable in the Temple of Set. Only if the Setian is known to be an ethical and responsible individual will his variance from social norms be tolerated.

Even so, it is a tenuous situation. We have tried not to err in the direction of paranoia. The ethical admonition in the *Crystal Tablet* is fairly succinct. We want every Setian to be aware of it. There are always wild rumors of Satanists sacrificing children or animals floating around, and we think it prudent to make it quite clear that the Temple of Set is not engaged in anything like that. We have never had to expel a member for anything like this, I am glad to say.

[Like the Church of Satan, the Temple of Set underwent a crisis as well. Although Aquino intended the Temple of Set to be the perfect initiatory organization by exploiting no one and offering every conceivable opportunity to everyone, things were going wrong. The Temple began to suffer shock after shock caused by senior initiates. Finally, in the summer of 1984, a conspiracy to pervert and degrade the Temple was barely exposed and stopped in time. Aquino believed the damage was devastating.]

DR. MICHAEL AQUINO: In about the year XIV (1979) I stepped down from the High Priesthood of Set, feeling that I had done my work to get the Temple off to a good start. I thought it would be healthy for the Temple to get into the habit of regarding the High Priesthood as an office which could be reassigned to various individuals as appropriate— rather than being regarded as a permanent/lifetime designation, as is the papacy for example.

The individual who was selected for the High Priesthood was an excellent, charismatic leader in many ways, but as time passed he grew increasingly insistent that the Temple's Initiates—and Priesthood—adhere to his own magickal point of view in a dogmatic way. This was in contradiction to the "free dialogue of ideas" which had previously characterized the Temple. When his increasingly restrictive policies clashed with the Bylaws, he abruptly resigned from the Temple shortly before the Conclave in the summer of XVII (1982). The Council of Nine reappointed me as High Priest; my intent was to get rid of the restrictive, regimented policies and then step aside in favor of another new High Priest.

Unfortunately a few members of the Priesthood—and two

Masters of the Temple—decided that they liked the dictatorial, dogmatic atmosphere. Seeing me tear it down, they attempted to seize control of the Temple by attacking me personally and by maneuvering to mislead the Council. One of the Priests whom they sought to enlist, however, blew the whole thing wide open at a Council meeting. A short time later the unethical individuals were expelled via the voting process specified in the Bylaws.

The significance of this was not just that a few power-hungry individuals engaged in cheap soap opera. Although there were only a few high-level Initiates who "went bad," the impact on some of the junior Initiates was severe. Some left in dismay; others simply waited on the sidelines for a while to see how the Temple would deal with this. It took about two years before the shock subsided and everyone felt comfortable again. We have since been operating once more in an open, non-dogmatic atmosphere. I would like to think that the soap opera is behind us for good, and that we can concentrate on more exalted visions.

[On Oct. 19, 1984, Aquino conducted a working in Wewelsburg Castle in Westphalia. The castle is used as a youth hostel except for a museum and two ceremonial chambers. The working took place in the Hall of the Dead, a *sanctum sanctorum* that Heinrich Himmler had constructed for his own Black Arts workings. Himmler was Adolf Hitler's head of the SS, and later of the Gestapo. Himmler began a campaign to build death camps around the same time that he became enamored with the occult. The purpose of Aquino's working was to obtain a full understanding of the significance of the crisis in the Temple. Aquino believed that Wewelsburg was conceived by Himmler to be the "Mittelpunkt der Welt" (center of the world), and the focus of the Hall of the Dead was to be the gate of that center and therefore a locus of the powers of darkness.]

Aquino later wrote: The reality of this chamber rushed in

upon me. This was no Hollywood set, no ordinary room painted and decorated to titillate the senses: 1,285 inmates of the Niederhagen concentration camp died during the reconstruction of the Wewelsburg for the SS. If the Marble Hall and the Walhalla (Hall of the Dead) were memorials to a certain unique quality in mankind, they also serve as grisly reminders of the penalty which mankind pays for that quality.

Where the Church of Satan and Temple of Set have appeared, so has the shadow of that signified by the Order been reflected. Now it has been loosed in its full force. Whether or not the sacred Priesthood continues to exist, the Order will do so; for its release is an inevitable legacy of the I-XVIII Working. Mankind received the utopian visions of the Church of Satan and the Temple of Set only as it strived to be worthy of them; it will continue to receive them only as it continues to prove itself worthy.

But the Order of the Trapezoid, whether known by its true name or by countless others, will always exist—not as a visible institution, but as a principle in the intelligent mind. Anton Szandor LaVey's Law of the Trapezoid will endure as well. Those who recognize the principle will be able to turn to it to their deliberate use; those who do not will nonetheless be subject to it.

DR. MICHAEL AQUINO: The working's most concrete result was the reactivation of the Order of the Trapezoid. I prefer not to discuss what I may feel to be its other results as they would tend to be incomprehensible to other than advanced magicians, just as advanced medical research would be to non-specialists in that field.

DET. SANDI GALLANT: The Temple of Set claims to be very intellectual and elite. I don't know about that. Based on people I've talked to from the Temple, that may not be true.

The OTO is another interesting group. They claim not to

be Satanic. OTO will claim to be ceremonial magick. I, however, would put them in with Satanic groups. They're pagan based, but pagans don't want to claim them.

Everyone worries about the Process Church because nobody knows much about them. They are based in Los Angeles, and I've heard unsubstantiated reports that they may be active in the Bay Area. Anyone who says they know where they really are doesn't know what they're talking about because nobody really knows. They're very, very secretive. [It has been alleged that Charles Manson and David Berkowitz, New York City's "Son of Sam" killer, were affiliated with the Process.]

CAPT. DALE GRIFFIS [from a lecture to police officers]: In traditional groups, members come from all ages, even second generation. Often they are of high intellect and good station in life. Doctors, lawyers, and even police officers have been known to be members. All are secretive in nature and act covertly. They are well organized. How many there are in these groups is unknown. Some networking among groups goes on.

Usually the activity is on known holidays. [There are four main occult holidays and four lesser holidays. Many of these holidays were observed by the Celts who believed in celebrating the holiday eves. The holidays are:

1. Halloween, also called Samhain, October 31, beginning of the Celtic year. The spirits are set free to roam the earth, a good time to contact spirits.

2. Beltane, also called May Eve and Walpurgisnacht, April 30. The time to begin planting crops. The Celts offered human sacrifices to ensure good food supply and fertility.

3. Summer Solstice, June 22, longest day of the year.

4. Winter Solstice, Yule, December 22, shortest day of the year.

5. Candlemas, February 2, beginning of the time for preparation for spring because the days are getting longer. Also called Feast of Ormelc.

6. Spring Equinox, March 21, day and night are the same length with days getting longer.

7. Lammas, August 1, beginning of harvest season.

8. Autumnal Equinox, September 21, day and night are the same length with days getting shorter.

As mentioned earlier, Satanists also celebrate their birthday as the most important day of the year.]

Persons use robes, knives, and other ritual items and use a book for recording their actions called a Book of Shadows.

Incest, animal mutilation and child pornography are often rumored to be part of their activities. Some members are marked with tattoos of Satanic symbols on the left side of the body. These groups seek solace and secrecy and will be found in areas where they feel they can be left alone.

The most dangerous groups are the ones that we know nothing about. They are usually generational and don't publicize their activities like the Church of Satan. They are the real underground.

DET. PAT METOYER: For the most part, people who join organized Satanic cults are white, upper-middle-class young people. You won't find many blacks. Why? Because he already knows that there's no such thing as a free meal. That no one will give you anything for nothing. But people who live in a very idealistic community feel, well possibly this is true because Mom and Dad are very successful. . . . Of course, if blacks or browns were to get into the occult or Black Arts they would be drawn to *Santeria* or something like that.

I met a Satanist at a Satanic baptism I attended. One parent of the baby they were going to baptize started asking me these questions in a very condescending manner. "What do you do? You're a policeman?" It was sort of like, "Can't you find anything else better?" I said, "What do you do?" He said, "I'm going to be an attorney." When he said attorney, I figured we had something in common, both on the side of law and order. I said, "Have you taken the bar yet?"

"No, not yet."

I said, "Are you studying for it?"

He said, "I don't have to study for it. I will just tell Satan that I am going to take the test, and I will pass it." I said, "Well, why haven't you taken it yet?"

He said, "Well, I've got a few more things to do to prepare, but whatever you tell Satan to do, he will do. He is powerful."

DET. SANDI GALLANT: The main reason why people get involved in Satanism is power and control. The other reason is that it gives them a presence.

[**"Phil"** is a thirty-five-year-old bus driver in the Chicago area. He asked that his full name not be used.]

PHIL: If you know anything about Satanism, you know it's about one thing—power. Power over yourself, power over others, power over your surroundings. How many people take that power? It's a power that we all have, but most of us are too scared to let loose, take control of the power that Satan has given us.

I like the fact that you don't grovel, you don't kneel and ask God for things. That, to me, is begging. My being is too proud for begging. You have to be real sure of yourself to be a Satanist. You have to have your act together.

I ask Satan for what I want! I don't beg some God that you can't see. Can I see Satan? You bet. Look at all the sickness, hurt, and warfare in the world. That's Satan. If there really was a God, and he's supposed to be so good, why does he let all these bad things happen? I'll tell you why. Because Satan takes charge here on earth, and God takes care of heaven. All good little people will go to heaven when they die. That's nice. I'm going to hell where I'm going to continue indulging myself. So, while you're being good so you can go to heaven after you die, I'm going to keep on enjoying myself here on earth and again in hell. Who's having the better time, me or you?

No, my group isn't affiliated with any established group. We're our own group. In fact, some of the people in our group had parents who were Satanists. We have a name, but I'm not telling you what it is. You wouldn't know what it meant, anyway. How many people? About fifty, at any one time. We break up into smaller groups for workings.

I won't tell you about our specific activities. That's secret, but I will tell you this: we do whatever we want, the people in our group. We have connections for anything. I'll leave it at that. If you think I'm going to admit illegal action to you, you're crazy.

DET. SANDI GALLANT: The second category of Satanists I call dabblers or fringe people. They are in little cult groups, sometimes individuals, not attached to any group. They tend to glean their ideology or philosophy from a variety of sources. Some label these people as self-styled Satanists. Many of these people, like "The Night Stalker," may have wanted to attach themselves to established groups, but nobody wanted them.

[Richard Ramirez is the alleged "Night Stalker," currently on trial for thirteen murders and forty-three felony counts ranging from rape to assault and battery. Ramirez told police he was a Satanist and flashed a pentagram inscribed in his left palm to reporters covering his arraignment, at which he pleaded innocent. Ramirez left the court shouting "Hail Satan."]

These fringe people tend to use the religion as a way of justifying their own criminal behavior, so they don't have to deal with any guilty feelings. In this category I would place Clifford St. Joseph.

[Clifford St. Joseph was convicted in March 1988 of first degree murder. During the trial, it was revealed that his victim had been drained of blood. St. Joseph faces a sentence of thirty-five years to life in prison.]

In June 1985, a man was found in the "meat rack" area. The perpetrators were gay and kept the guy in a cage and used him sexually. They carved a pentagram in his chest. Boyd Stephens, the medical examiner, found candlewax drippings in the right eye. He was John Doe #60 and still is, I believe, unidentified.

The alleged killer and his associates had all the books. They were typical dabblers. They were studying the Crowley books, Regardie, LaVey. They had the amulets. They were into a self-styled form. The only reason for this homicide was a ritual that we could see. I don't believe they made any attempt to join the Church of Satan, but there was evidence that they had been in touch with the OTO.

The majority of crimes that we're seeing that we have evidence for fall within this category. With organized groups, it's very deliberate that we're not finding any evidence of criminal activity. They're much too careful and hide their tracks very well.

The third category would be the youth subculture. I categorize this differently than fringe people, because these kids may be playing with it more than anything else. A small percentage will carry it beyond that level. These kids are often influenced by heavy metal music or by fantasy role playing games like Dungeons & Dragons. The kids who go beyond the normal curiosity tend to be those who have other behavior problems going on—problems in school, with peers, at home, and of course they have that desire for power and control. In this group I would put Sean Sellars.

[In October 1986, an Oklahoma jury found Sean Sellars, seventeen, guilty of three counts of murder for killing his mother, stepfather and a convenience store clerk in the fall of 1985. Sellars was a self-styled Satanist who was obsessed with using human blood in his rituals. He kept several vials hidden in his refrigerator for black masses. He often carried it to school and drank it in the cafeteria in front of classmates.

A friend of Sellars's in Colorado, before Sellars moved to Oklahoma, testified at his trial that Sellars had formed a Satanic group called "The Elimination." The witness stayed in touch with Sellars through letters and phone calls from Colorado. During a visit back to Colorado by Sellars, the friend testified that he and Sellars wore black robes, drank their own blood, and conducted the candle-lit initiation into Satanism of a third boy. They cut the boy with an athame and used his blood to write a dedication to Satan.

During his trial, Sellars told of how he held a ceremony in his room, alone, in which he wrote in his own blood: "I renounce God, I renounce Christ, I will serve only Satan. Hail Satan!" He became addicted to Satanic rituals, often staying up late into the night practicing and reading about them. On September 8, 1985, he and another friend, Richard Howard —both had engaged in Satanic rituals together—held one last ritual before setting out for a human sacrifice. Sellars stole his grandfather's .357 Magnum and shot convenience store clerk Robert Bower, who had once refused to sell beer to Sellars.

Sellars became even more obsessed with Satanism and wrote shortly afterward in a school essay read during his trial, "Satanism made me a better person. . . . I can kill without remorse, and I feel no regret or sorrow, only love, compassion, hate, anger, pain, and joy. Only I may understand, but that is enough."

Sellars began arguing with his parents over a fifteen-year-old girl whom they forbade him to see. He ran away from home but returned. One night, after going home from his part-time job at a pizza store, he performed his nightly Satanic ritual. After drifting in and out of sleep that night he walked quietly into his parents' room and shot them both in the head. He went to his friend Richard Howard's house where he stashed the weapon. The next morning he made believe that he found his parents' bodies and didn't know what happened.

Howard testified for the prosecution and received a five-year sentence as an accessory after the fact. He claimed that he didn't take part in the clerk's murder but waited outside for his friend. Sellars is now the youngest inmate on Oklahoma's Death Row.]

The second and third groups are usually the most criminally destructive. We've recently seen increased activity among the third group. That activity will usually be homicide of parents or suicide.

The second category worries me the most because when you have an individual, like the Night Stalker, you're dealing with a mobile criminal, and agencies aren't necessarily networking with each other about it and exchanging information about these particularly bizarre crimes.

CAPT. DALE GRIFFIS: Self-styled Satanists are often identified as loners who have a criminal or sociopathic background. Examples are Son of Sam, Night Stalker, and other serial murderers. These people are dedicated and calculating and should not be underestimated.

Self-styled Satanists may also start their own occult group, taking bits and pieces from many occult religions. Manson is a good example. Followers are held in the group by drugs, mind control, intimidation, and the cult of confession. [This is where the leader will demand that members perform a criminal activity, such as murder, together. It binds the group with an *esprit de corps* but also brings newcomers past the point of leaving the group because they have committed a felony.] During their criminal acts, terms or unusual sayings are left with symbols which to them have meaning. Manson's group left HELTER SKELTER.

The last group I call the youthful experimenters. They are confused by adolescent anxiety and seek power to overcome it. They believe they can get power through occult ceremonies and actions. They seek powerful role models like heavy metal rock stars who cultivate occult trappings.

["James" is a self-styled Satanist living in Los Angeles. He is eighteen.]

JAMES: I got into Satanism about three years ago through some friends at school. We hold rituals every Friday night and on special holidays.

What I like about Satanism is the power that it gives me. The people at school know I'm into it, and they don't mess with me. It gives me the power to escape police when I have to. [James was arrested one year ago for burglary. He was given probation.] It also gives me the feeling that I can do anything I put my mind to.

The other religions don't teach that. They teach you to be humble and love one another. Why should I love anyone else? All people want is to get as much as they can. That's the way life is. Satanism has taught me about life. It helps you grow up.

DEPUTY PROBATION OFFICER DARLYNE PETTINICCHIO: I ask kids how they get into Satanism, and they tell me, I've read the Christian Bible. It tells me don't do this, don't do this, don't do this. It says everything I do is wrong, and if I live by that I'm going to burn in hell. I've read *The Satanic Bible*, and it says I can do anything I want. It gives me permission to have sex with anyone, and if I want to steal I can have anything I want. If I live by that Bible, I'm going to rule in hell. Kids say, I'm going to hell either way. I may as well rule there.

These kids have no sense of a forgiving God. If you've done something wrong, you've had it. There's no going back.

I think a lot of the music portrays that. We have kids who act out the "Oath." To many kids it starts out as a fad. This is no big deal. This is cool. They're not really into Satanism, but some get carried away. Then it's dangerous.

Kids are so into the power between good and evil. The stuff they write in their notebooks, for instance, the pact with Satan, the Oath:

"My Lord and Master Satan, I acknowledge you as my God and Prince and promise to serve and obey you while I live. I renounce the other God and Jesus Christ, the saints, the church of Rome and all its sacraments, and prayers that the faithful may offer me. I promise to do as much evil as I can, and draw others to evil. I renounce chrism, baptism, and all the merits of Jesus Christ and his saints, and if I should fail to serve and adore you, paying you homage, I give you my life as your own."

DET. SANDI GALLANT: One thing I've noticed from the calls I get is that Satanism tends to be more suburban than it is urban. The kids there for the most part tend to be from better families economically. The kids can pretty much do what they want. They get real bored, need something to fill their time, and unfortunately it's not always something healthy. They're getting double messages at home. They're at a rebellious age. One of the biggest problems is the society we live in. Very negative, violent, and kids perceive it as normal.

[Tim Boyle is an officer for the Maryland National Capital Park Police in Montgomery County, Maryland. He became interested in the occult because of a case in which a child's body was dug up by a group of teenagers led by a self-proclaimed Satanist. He has begun teaching park police officers about occult activities so that they can recognize it when it comes. Because his agency's jurisdiction is county parks and surrounding areas his colleagues are beginning to see a lot of occult-related activity.]

OFFICER TIM BOYLE: Sometimes it's difficult to know what you're dealing with when you see a crime scene. We find that Anton LaVey's Church of Satan has been bastardized through people's own interpretations and definitions. Sometimes we see a lot of Crowley mixed in. You're not going to find anything set in stone. You may not only find black and white candles being used. You may find other colors. I worked one case where a kid said he was both God and the Devil. That's something Manson would say.

Don't fool yourself. People who are into the occult are intelligent and well read. They study. They take the basics of Satanism and embellish it. Sometimes it's all over the place, but sometimes it's very precise.

DET. CLEO WILSON: You can often tell how deep someone is into the occult by the things they have. That separates the dabblers from the self-styled Satanist from the organized folks. If you're just curious about the subject you don't go out and buy all the robes, chalices and so on. That stuff is expensive. If you're just dabbling you don't buy the expensive items. Another indication is books. People who have a lot of books are serious. It takes a lot of effort to study books.

DET. BILL WICKERSHAM: Many people are building their own belief systems. They're pulling from this book and from that book. It's hard to be an expert because it changes overnight. It's like juvenile gangs. You can be an expert one day, then tomorrow it's something totally different. We do have a profile of someone who joins Satanic groups. We were at a lecture and they handed out Sandi's profile, and it was exactly the same as ours. It freaked me out. The list was this: loner, above average IQ, underachiever, strives for control or power, takes drugs, preoccupation with death, pornographic material, secretive. Of course doing one, two, or even three of these things doesn't make you a Satanist. It's more like the other way around. Satanists, especially teens, have these characteristics.

OFFICER TIM BOYLE: I look at the graffiti. It tells you which groups are operating in your area. Sometimes it even tells you the names of the members of the group, just like gangs. Depending upon which Satanic graffiti you see, you can tell what part of the occult craft they're into.

[Judy Hanson is an attorney's investigator in Southern California. She has investigated cases of sexual abuse in Southern California day-care centers in which the victims claimed the adults employed Satanic rituals as part of the abuse.]

JUDY HANSON: The more I look at this, the more I keep telling people that you can't always apply logic and order to something so illogical as this. The reason why some people get into Satanism is that there doesn't have to be a structure. People are free to make up their own rules.

CHAPTER SIX:

WITCHCRAFT
AND SATANISM

Most modern day practitioners of Witchcraft cringe when the words Satanism and Witchcraft are used in the same sentence. Witchcraft means different things to different people, and unfortunately for followers of the "old religion," it's often taken to be synonymous with Satanism.

The reason for that is simple. During the Middle Ages, the term witch was often used to describe anyone who was a heretic and, to the thinking of church clergy, in league with the Devil. That notion still sticks today. How the practices of the old religion turned into heresy isn't clear, but some scholars suggest it was due to misplaced enthusiasm by Inquisitors who believed that anyone who wasn't a Christian, who worshiped other deities, had to be against the church.

Contemporary followers of Witchcraft reject all of these medieval notions about their religion. They say theirs is a bona fide alternative faith, much of which predates the Catholic Church.

Defining contemporary Witchcraft isn't easy because there is no central group or strict body of beliefs that is shared by all. The strongest, most stable group in Witchcraft is the local coven, grove, or clan. Each is autonomous and able to form and follow its own belief system. For most who practice the craft, there are some common themes however: worship of nature and natural phenomena and the use of rituals.

[Gwyn Gwynallen leads a small Witchcraft clan in the Baltimore, Maryland, area.]

GWYN GWYNALLEN: Wicca, the name often given to modern Witchcraft, grew out of Great Britain from the writings of two people, Gerald Gardner and Alex Sanders. Those two branches of Witchcraft or paganism, to our minds, are wiccan. The rituals, customs, theological perspectives and so forth that go along with it are wiccan. Today, with all the books out about Witchcraft and festivals, people tend to form their own groups and their traditions on a whim and call it wicca. So the word *wicca* has become synonymous with all kinds of Witchcraft, but when people say they are wicca it may or may not derive from Gardner or Sanders. Our group, because we don't derive from those two, doesn't consider ourselves wiccan.

[Gerald Gardner was a retired customs official who dabbled in spiritualism and had a flair for the occult and unorthodox sexual tastes. He was a sado-masochist, exhibitionist, and voyeur. Gardner wanted to combine his needs into a witch cult and asked Aleister Crowley to help him compose rituals. They both belonged to OTO at the time.

Gardner's witchcraft was practiced only by Gardner and a few close friends until 1954 when he published *Witchcraft Today*, in which he claimed that witch cults existed and that he was involved with them. He received a torrent of letters and requests to join the coven and within a few years covens were operating all over England.

Gardnerian witchcraft was brought to the U.S. by Raymond Buckland and his wife, Rosemary, who met Gardner in England and were initiated into the craft. Each coven is headed by a high priestess and high priest. A high priestess is mandatory for a ritual to take place, but a high priest is not.

Membership is by couples and limited to the number of people who can fit into a nine-foot circle. New covens are formed when a witch leaves a full coven and starts a new one. Gardnerians hold rituals skyclad, and the high priest and priestess wear bracelets showing their rank. The witch-queen wears a crown and garter.

Alex Sanders said he was initiated as a witch when he was seven years old by his grandmother who was a witch. As the story goes, she had him stand nude in a circle with his head down. She took a sharp razor, cut his scrotum to make it bleed slightly, and declared him a witch. He was initiated as a third degree, and he became a black magickian. As with Gardner, media exposure spread his word. In 1969, a London newspaper published an article about Sanders and turned him into a celebrity. He also went on many TV shows. Alexandrian Witchcraft is noted for its use of sexual intercourse—real and symbolic—for initiation rites.]

GWYN GWYNALLEN: We practice Shamani Witchcraft. We are monists. We believe in a single life force within which a great deal of diversity abounds and within which the God and Goddess exist. We address our invocations to something more like a Native American "great spirit." We think of ourselves as equal with nature.

[Margot Adler is a journalist for National Public Radio and author of *Drawing Down the Moon*, a comprehensive book about Witchcraft. She currently does not belong to an organized Witchcraft group but has in the past. She describes herself as a pagan.]

MARGOT ADLER: *Wicca* has become a ubiquitous term, and it's being used by a bunch of different groups. Some follow the ideas of Gardner and Sanders but others don't. Some think they're not following Gardner or Sanders and really are. Some people just go the library, read a lot of books, form a group, and think they're witches. Wicca is the revival and re-creation of Western European Paganism but very much influenced by Gerald Gardner and others. The women's movement appropriated the word *wicca* for the whole female spirituality movement. There's been a large cross-fertilization.

I was powerfully affected by the Greek goddesses when I was in school. I got very into the Greek mythology. I really believed, when I was a teenager, that if I had any religion it would have been the ancient Greek religions. When I got to be fourteen, I realized it was crazy. People just don't do that anymore. Adults just don't believe in the Greek gods. The feminist images, however, were very strong for me.

I used to call myself a witch. I thought it was a matter of pride to reclaim the name. But I find myself in recent years less comfortable with the name *witch*, mainly because it takes three hours to explain what the word means. It would be nice to reclaim the word, but I don't feel optimistic that can happen in this day and age. I am more comfortable with the word *pagan*.

[Just as nuns may take religious names when they enter the convent, so do those who enter the realm of Witchcraft. Feather is the magickal name of a witch in southern Ohio. Now thirty-seven, she has practiced the art since she was a teenager. She assists law enforcement authorities in her area on occult crime.]

FEATHER: If you're a Christian you believe in Satan. We don't believe in Satan as an entity or anything else. We see mischievous spirits. We see dark-side entities, but we don't see Satan as an entity.

We see the Goddess and the God. The Goddess is represented by the moon. The God, or the Lord, is represented by the sun. They each rule six months out of the year. We call them Mother Moon and Father Sun. We do see an overseeing deity above them both. We see the Goddess and God as the right and left hands of this overseeing deity.

We are not Satanists. I can say that a million times and people still won't understand the difference. Satanists are destructive people. Their religion is destructive. Our motto is "Do what thou wilt, but harm ye none." That takes in all the Ten Commandments.

There is a natural curiosity about the occult. There always has been. I was into it very young, but I never went for the dark side. I didn't think it was my calling. I knew from my Christian upbringing that killing things was wrong. When my coven came about, it didn't advocate killing. I knew this was right. I felt comfortable with it.

In our history there were sacrifices to God just as there were in the Christian religion. It was stopped way back when, just as it was stopped in religions like Christianity and Judaism.

DR. JEFFREY RUSSELL: There are just about as many witchcraft religions as there are groups. They shift and change constantly. Generically, the main types you'll find are the ones that go back to the old gods. They may be attracted to Egyptian or Greek mythology.

The other type that's quite common is the feminist type of Witchcraft. The emphasis is on the Goddess and not the God. They see the Goddess as the center of their devotion in opposition to the traditional paternalistic religions.

DR. CARL RASCHKE: The purpose of wicca is to preserve the old religion, the so-called Goddess religion. Eighty percent of those who say they practice wicca really don't, because so much is improvised on the spot. A lot of the people in wicca, mostly women, are members of the literati who read about medieval romance and renaissance folk culture and so forth who kind of created their own rituals and call them authentic.

MARGOT ADLER: This is an incredibly anarchistic movement. There are very few dogmas. That could be why it's so popular.

You do, however, find that people who practice Witchcraft have common ideas. There is the use of ritual but not necessarily ritual magick in the strict sense of the word. We're not talking about conjuring spirits. Some groups lean towards an occult bent and some don't. There is a wish to attune oneself to natural cycles. Definitely.

They are an incredibly bookish lot, a lot of ties with science fiction and fantasy. There used to be a theory—which turned out to be disproved—that half the people in the pagan movement were ex-Catholics and high Episcopalians who loved the ritual but didn't want the dogma. As it turned out, studies have shown the profile of those in Witchcraft mirrored that of American religions. Most of the people have a love of ceremony, love of ritual, love of imagination, and a deep desire for roots.

You don't have a large number of blacks and Hispanics in this movement. They would go to *Santeria* or something else. A lot of white Westerners feel they are bereft of a real culture. They don't have the stories or the songs like Native Americans or the Jews or any ethnic group. They want to go back and figure out what their Welsh, Irish and Italian ancestors were doing. There's a desperate search for roots among these white Westerners. That's behind a lot of the movement in Witchcraft and Paganism.

When I became interested in this, I tried writing to various groups. I knew the code words. They signed their letters Blessed Be and they would use words like *wicca* and *craft*. The first thing I saw was an ad in the Village Voice for a shop called Blessed Are The Blessed Be. I went there, but it turned out to be run by The Church of Satan. I went in, and it didn't feel right. I ran into a woman there who called herself Wally the Witch or something. It was ridiculous.

DR. CARL RASCHKE: In principle, Satanism and wicca are not the same, but I like to use this story to show what can happen to some, certainly not all, people who practice Witchcraft.

You go to a fancy ball strutting around in your formal gowns and act very proper, but sometimes it gets a little rowdy and you end up at an orgy in the back room. That orgy in the back room is what Satanism is. Some of the neo-pagan groups are recruiting grounds for Satanism. Very often, people who become high in wicca decide that they want to be even more powerful. This whole business of manipulating energy, zapping your enemies, and so forth which goes on, taken one step further becomes Satanism.

CAPT. DALE GRIFFIS: I know about white witchcraft and black Witchcraft, but you can't tell me that every once in a while a white witch doesn't get a little taste of the power he or she has conjured and takes it just a step further.

DET. BILL WICKERSHAM: We were in California, in Anaheim, going to a seminar. It was February 1986. When we came back, we got this call about a man who was stabbed 114 times by a woman. The detective in homicide who was handling the case had gone to one of our seminars. He said there were signs of Satan worship there. The detective must have been half asleep during the lecture, because we told him specifically that Witchcraft is not Satanism. There were signs of Witchcraft at the scene. There were signs of worshiping a deity, the Goddess, but not Satan.

We went through the material and said there's a lot of Witchcraft here and that we'd like to see the body. We went to the morgue to see the body and spoke to Dr. Thomas, the coroner, who is very knowledgeable about ritualistic crime. He thought it was a ritualistic homicide, and so did we.

The woman had called the police and said, "I have a man

tied up on my bed, and if you don't come and get him, I'm going to kill him." They thought they had a nut on the phone. She called back again, "I'm going to kill this son of a bitch if you don't get over here." The dispatchers wrote it off as a kook. The woman finally called a girlfriend who called an attorney, and when the police finally got over there she's in there with a knife and there's blood all over the place, and this guy is lying there with 114 stab wounds.

There was a *D* carved on his chest with a line through it. I don't know if it was an arrow or what. He had little 7s all the way around the *D*. I can only guess about the 7s because I didn't get to talk to her. It may have something to do with Crowley's book, *Liber* 777. [In magick, 7 is considered the most mysterious and one of the most important numbers. Traditionally, the seventh son of the seventh son has magickal powers. Many occultists believe that the number 7 governs life cycles and completeness: seven days in a week, seven notes in the musical scale, seven planets (to the ancients), seven colors in the spectrum, seven deadly sins, the moon's cycle is made up of four phases, each lasting seven days.]

As for the *D*, it could stand for Dana, her name, or something completely different. This homicide went down around Candlemas during which fertility rituals go on—sex magick. Too many things came together. There were two girls involved, and they said they were lesbians. The suspect kept saying, "We are in the AA."

I said to Cleo, "Where have we heard about AA before, Cleo? We've either read it or heard it." It turns out it was at a seminar. AA was an offshoot of Crowley's magick. [Crowley set up a sex magick group called *Astrum Argentium* (silver star) or AA in 1907.]

Homicide detectives handled this all wrong. They called us for consultation, and then wouldn't let us see all the material. [The detectives directly involved would not talk about the case.] They said when they got there the girl had blood in her mouth. I said, "Did you pump her stomach, get a sample? Maybe she was drinking urine and eating feces." He said to me, "For what!"

I said, "Did you ask the coroner to check the guy?"

"For what, he's got one hundred fourteen stab wounds."

I said, "You don't know. The coroner can find many things that you can't."

Sure enough. There was blood in the guy's gut. It was consumed, not from the stab wounds. That tells you what was going on. I say there was a blood ritual and sex magick ritual. She had bound him. Evidently, they were snorting coke and drinking wine. I heard that he might have been involved in Satanism, but I haven't confirmed it.

There was a little altar in the basement with candles, the whole bit. At the foot of the bed on the floor she had a dish with a pentagram in it. There were a lot of herbs around. Satanists don't use a lot of herbs. People involved in Witchcraft do. There were a lot of books about the occult in the area.

We found out her dad sexually abused her, possibly an uncle, too. The dad and uncle had inverted pentagrams tattooed on their arms, she said. You tell me what was going on. The bottom line is I think they were doing a sex ritual and she lost it. She just lost it.

I can't get involved in the case because if I did I can get cited for getting involved in another man's case. They asked for our help, then didn't give us a chance to follow through.

The girl was written off to crazy. She's doing Pueblo. [Mental health facility at Pueblo, Colorado.]

FEATHER: A lot of people look upon witches as Devil worshipers. They don't see the difference, and they don't understand the difference. All they see is something black, something dark, and that's not what it is. They've been told this; it's been drilled into their heads. You can't blame them.

When the first animal mutilations occurred in the county

in which I live they said the witches did it. That's when we got up in arms. We said wait a minute. . . . A police officer called me and said that he had been told to talk with me. I explained the situation, told him what we did, and we have been working together ever since. I act as consultant to the police on the occult.

Yes, I have to admit that some Witchcraft groups do sacrifice animals to get more power. In any group of people you'll get that sort of behavior. We don't condone it and we don't like it.

[Some police are beginning to understand Witchcraft groups and their need to hold ceremonies outside. Some do not.]

OFFICER TIM BOYLE: There are a lot of witchcraft groups that use the parks for their ceremonies. In general, as long as they don't destroy any property or bother anyone else, we leave them alone. Their activities are protected by law.

CONTRA COSTA COUNTY (CA) CASE FILE # R87-12732

SUSPICIOUS CIRCUMSTANCES
LOCATION: 616 MINER ROAD, ORINDA
SUNDAY 5-24-87 1230

SYNOPSIS: This report concerns listed individuals performing religious ceremonies in a secluded wooded area while wearing white robes.

DESCRIPTION: At approximately 1230 hrs, V. Lai phoned sheriff's office radio and requested an officer concerning strange individuals near his home. Upon arrival V. Lai said he noticed individuals on a hillside wearing white sheets. He felt the Ku Klux Klan was having a meeting.

Using binoculars, I looked at a hillside to the west of V. Lai's home. Among heavy brush I saw a small clearing approx. 20' dia. I saw three individuals dressed in what appeared to be KKK garments except the faces of each individual were not covered. The garments were all white from shoulders to feet. The cap was pointed at the top. The cap had a tail that hung down the back of the head to the shoulder area.

Each of the individuals walked slowly in a circle around a small fire.

Via radio, I requested EBRP [East Bay Regional Parks] helicopter Eagle 1 to survey the area (for officer safety reasons) prior to me hiking up the hill through brush.

Eagle 1 arrived and reported the individuals were not in the clearing. Eagle 1 could not see down through the heavy brush/trees. I hiked up to the clearing and found an area where tall poles had been erected in a semi-circle.

There was no apparent use/need for the poles erected in this manner. I found several bushes that had been enclosed with chicken wire and their base area hoed and watered. A small fire pit had been built with stone and cement. The area had a water hose and an electric cord that came from an unknown location to the west. The area appeared to be a club or religious meeting area. I walked westward and found "steps" which descended down the hill. The steps were cut into the earth.

Halfway down the hill I found a small wood shack 12' × 12'. Through a window I saw a bed (no mattress) on the floor and a chair.

At the bottom of the trail I exited the hillside foliage on the driveway of 616 Miner Rd. Three individ-

uals were in front of the res. garage. I explained the
above info. Emmon Bodfish WFA [white female adult]
explained that she is a Reformed Druid of North
America Celtic Group. Bodfish said they were performing religious ceremonies.

Bodfish explained that ceremonies are held at
various locations. Bodfish provided religious information about her group.

—Report is for info only—
Reporting deputy: John Rock

MARGOT ADLER: I was at a festival in Oregon three years
ago. It was all women, about three hundred, mostly singing
and so on. Two police officers wandered around, saw some
pentagrams, some of the signals, and they ended up telling
reporters that there was Satanic stuff going on. There was
nothing, nothing.

CHAPTER SEVEN:

HISPANIC
WITCHCRAFT

What Westerners think of as Witchcraft can be traced to European roots. There is a large body of Witchcraft, unique to the Americas, however, which bears no resemblance at all to European Witchcraft.

The most practiced occult art is called Santeria, which in Spanish means "worship of the saints." Adherents are called Santeros. The religion has its roots in African tribal religions found among the Yoruba people in southwestern Nigeria. Their belief system revolves around the worship of many deities, each of whom is responsible for a different aspect of day-to-day life on earth. Each god has its own colors, numbers, special powers and personality. These deities are worshiped during elaborate ceremonies. Believers sacrifice animals, offer fruits, flowers, or a god's favorite items to get his or her attention and favor. The larger the sacrifice, the larger the favor—or solution to a problem—asked.

When the Yoruba were brought to the New World as slaves, they brought their religion with them. Slave owners insisted that they give up their beliefs, however, and convert to Christianity. The slaves found a way around it. While seeming to pray to the Catholic saints, they actually were praying to their own gods. What evolved was a syncretization of Catholic saints and tribal gods. Although there are hundreds of gods, seven particular ones, known as Orishas, are the most revered. Although the Yoruba openly practice their religion in

Africa, the rituals practiced in the Americas are closed to out-siders.

Variations of Santeria *are found all over the Caribbean and the Americas. In Haiti, it mixed with Catholicism and the beliefs of the Fon people from Dahomey to form Voodoo. In Brazil, there are offshoots known as* Candomble, Um-banda, *and* Macumba. *In Cuba, you find* Santeria *sects of* Abaqua *and* Palo Mayombe.

The majority of Santeros *are law-abiding. The most common conflict with law enforcement comes with the practice of killing animals during sacrifices. Laws in some states are changing to accommodate these religious practices, however.*

The animal sacrifices, though, are insignificant when compared with the human sacrifices, drug trafficking and other felonies that are being committed by people using Santeria *practices before, during, and after the crimes in addition to those using* Santeria *as an excuse to commit these crimes. This is especially true in areas with high concentrations of* Marielitos—*Cuban refugees, many of whom were hardcore criminals from Castro's prisons—who entered the United States in 1980 during the famous boatlift.*

DET. PAT METOYER: If you look at *Santeria*, it's like Witch-craft in that Witchcraft is neither white nor black. It's gray, if you will, because the person officiating is going to determine the kind of magick that's going to be used. *Santeria* is a gray magick. Within the Santeria cult there is something called *Palo Mayombe*, however, which is the darkest side. Generi-cally, witches are called *Brujas*, but those who deal in the darkest side are called *Palo Mayomberos*. They do curses and spells and that kind of deviant behavior.

CAPT. DALE GRIFFIS: When I first started lecturing, one of the first places I spoke was the Ohio Peace Officers Academy in London, Ohio. I spoke about non-traditional groups. I spoke to them about *Santeria* and told them about Sandi's case with Leroy Carter. [The headless corpse found in Golden Gate Park, Chapter 2.] I said that we really didn't have *Santeria* around here. That's what I thought, but the officers began telling me about finding chickens lying around, about finding feathers with coins lying around. That's when we realized that the *Marielitos* were infiltrating the Mexicanos in the foreign labor movement in Ohio.

Subsequently, I found that a lot of departments in Northwest Ohio had been receiving reports of alleged activity which appeared to be *Santeria*. For the first time, these guys knew what pigeonholes to put these things into.

[Jack Frasier is the pseudonym of a detective in a large Midwestern city. He asked that his name not be used and his city not identified because his department does not permit him to discuss occult crime. He has been a police officer for more than twenty years.]

DET. JACK FRASIER: We had a case around here not too long ago where police found a bunch of goats slaughtered, and the papers immediately called it Satanic. They called me, and I said, "Describe the room to me." They described the goats and blood and I said, "Is there anything else there?" They said there were statues, and they described the statues. I said, "Is there any money around?" They said yes. There was money hanging on strings and like that. I told them it was *Santeria*.

You got to know the difference between them. Right away it's Satanic, Satanic, Satanic. It doesn't make things any better; that's for sure, but at least you know what you're dealing with, and you can go ahead with your investigation in the right direction. It all comes with training.

OFFICER TIM BOYLE: In the Washington area there are a

lot of Cubans and other Hispanics. There's a great deal of *Santeria*, *Brujeria*, *Palo Mayombe*. It's all something we as police officers should know about.

I got a call from another agency that they found a Satanic site. I went down there, and there was a tongue—looked like a cow's tongue—nailed to a tree with a screwdriver. It had been there a while. At the base of it was a T-shirt, pair of pants, pair of socks, pair of shoes and underwear—everything a person would be wearing. There were seven coins, a Cuban cigar, and a dead bird. The officer said to me, "There must be Satanists around here. Let's try to find them."

I said, "To tell you the truth, I would be looking more into the dope angle. Somebody is in fear of somebody else telling the police something about their organization or their drug smuggling or something along those lines."

I said, "Instead of looking around for a bunch of people worshiping Satan we should be looking for a bunch of Cubans that are selling drugs in the apartment complex right behind us."

That's what it turned out to be.

Another time, I got a call from one of our officers who acted like he had seen a ghost. It was three o'clock in the morning, he was driving along the road, crossing some railroad tracks, he looks down and sees two candles on the tracks inside a bag. He looks in the bag, and there's a mutilated piece of meat. It looked like a roast.

He figures they must have just been here because the candles were still lit. It turned out to be some Cubans worshiping the iron god [Oggun]. It pays to look at this stuff, and it also pays not to discount anything. Sure, you take the meat and send it to the lab to make sure it's a roast or whatever it is. It could be something else. You never know, but hopefully I'm good enough to know what I'm saying. I've talked to others about it, and we decided that it was someone worshiping the iron god.

DET. SANDI GALLANT: After we had the Leroy Carter homicide, which we believed to be *Santeria*, we began to look at the botanicas. People get confused when they walk into botanicas, bookstores that *Santerians* will go into, because they see all these Catholic saints in there. They think it's a store where they have Catholic artifacts. But as you go in, you see all this occult kind of stuff. Of course, *Santeria* is a combination of the religions. We had two stores in San Francisco, both in the Mission District. One was called Botanica Aruba. I've been in there a couple of times talking to the people. I would call it kind of an okay place to go. The people were fairly helpful and pretty nice.

Another one was called the Santa Barbara Candle Shop. The name has significance in *Santeria*. [Saint Barbara is syncretized to Chango, the god of fire, thunder and lightning. He oversees warriors and his punishment is death. See chart (p. 266) for other gods and their powers and functions.] That was on 24th St. We had a black officer who went into that place, on a case, and when he came back he said, "That place is scary. I don't want to go back in there."

Every time we would go out there, we thought they had a look-see man. It was like going to a gambling house. There's always that one guy outside. That's how this place was. As a Caucasian, there was no way I could go into that place. They knew I didn't belong there. I doubt that too many people went in there that they didn't know. We were interested in them for a while in connection with some of our *Santeria* cases.

I remember one surveillance where we followed one of the women who came out of there. We had two cars following her, another detective and me. Jerry was still watching the store. It was at night.

She pulled over on the freeway, just pulled over. We were way back. On the freeway, it's real easy to follow someone especially at night. We think she was probably going to a cemetery to get some dirt. [Cemetery dirt is often used in

Santeria rituals.] She was going down a road that nobody ever takes. Knowing that nobody ever takes that road, there is no way that we can follow her without burning ourselves. She's already hinky because she pulled over on the freeway. So we had to let her go, ended up losing her. There is nothing down there but cemeteries. There's another exit farther down that leads to houses, and we went all over looking for her car and didn't find it.

Our speculation was that she went to the cemeteries to get dirt. There were no gates up and at that time of night you can just drive through. We had her identified. We had most of the people who were involved with the store identified. Most of them were Mariel boat people.

DET. PAT METOYER: We have a case going on now of a man being coerced into becoming part of a Colombian dope ring. He is forty-three years old and is from Colombia. He's a used car salesman. He's going to L.A. City College to brush up on his English and business.

He met a young girl there, also from Colombia, and they began talking. She says that she has a friend who would be interested in meeting our man. He's thinking of selling a car, and says to the girl that her friend should call him.

The fellow calls and asks, "How would you like to make some money, big money. All you have to do is deal cocaine." Our man says no.

The other man says, "I'm sure you'll probably come around."

One night someone bangs on his door. He opens it and sees a small doll. The doll has a nail driven through the ear.

The next day, the guy calls and says, "Do you want to do business?" Our man is still firm; he doesn't want to.

Two days later, there's another doll outside his house with a large phallus stuck up the doll's anal cavity. This guy's starting to get worried. How do we come into the case? The fellow then threatens to blow up his house, and our man calls the police and makes a crime report.

The next night, the night after calling the police, this fellow opens his door and finds a paper bag with eyes and mouth cut out of it. Inside is a candle. It is circled with salt and shaving cream leads from the circle of salt into the street. He says that's a sign that there is a *bruja*, a witch, who wants to get him. He says later that he didn't tell this to the police but prior to that a piece of liver was nailed to his door. He knows from the community in Colombia that he is from that *Santeria* is a big thing, and he is worried.

Our man is still out there. He's still scared. He is having some pains, but they are pains of a mental origin. He is suffering a psychic assault. He is having chest pains. He believes all this. He hasn't given in to them, but I'm not sure he can hold on.

Now what's a police department supposed to do? There's nothing we can do. Unless this person calls and says, "I'm going to put a bomb in your house," and we can prove he made the threat, there's nothing that a police agency can do. Nothing. Legally all we can do is watch it. Is it a crime to nail liver to someone's door? A guy leaves a doll on your front doorstep with a nail in the head to give you earaches . . . what crime is that? The people who do these things know that there's nothing we can do.

I have a voodoo doll that I use in my lectures. It was sent [originally] to a lady in the west end of town. Her old man is with the diplomatic corps. He, in fact, has a girlfriend, and he wants to sever his relationship with his wife. She doesn't want to get divorced, so he tells his girlfriend that his wife won't release him. She says, "Don't worry about it. I have an aunt who has some powers who will fix it."

Just before Christmas in 1985 the wife, her name is Joy, receives on her front doorstep a shoe box wrapped in aluminum. There's a great big red ribbon around it. It says, "Merry Christmas, Joy." Obviously she gets a little paranoid. After all, who is going to bring her a gift and leave it on the doorstep? She calls the police. The police respond and work on the assumption that it is a bomb, because her husband is with the diplomatic corps. They cut it open and inside is a doll, a little black-faced doll with the name "Joy" written across. There are pins in the throat, breast, stomach, and the vaginal area. There are five little black stones around the doll and one white candle in the head. The five stones stand for the five Orishas, the five little gods. [Although most *Santeros* worship seven Orishas, some only recognize five.]

She's very concerned, and the more she tries to relate to the officers what the problem is . . . she starts to lose her voice. She says, "It's hard for me to talk. I have something stuck in my throat." There's nothing we can do. There's no crime. I took the box and the doll and went back to the office.

About three hours later, I get a call and the person who answered our phone thinks someone is playing a joke because the voice is so low. I get on the phone and hear, "Mister Metoyer . . ." in this very faint, raspy voice. It's the wife.

I said, "Listen, here's what I'll do. I have some powers . . . I'll take the pins out. You tell me how it feels. I'm twisting it . . . now." I'm not doing anything, in fact. She screams, "Oh, it hurts." I say to her, "Okay, I'm pulling it . . . I'm pulling it . . . it's out!" I said, "I hope you feel better." She says, "I can breathe again. The pressure is released."

The powers that people can exert on others by this little doll, and play on people's minds is enormous. This lady in fact believed that had those pins not been taken out she was going to die. As it turned out, she left her old man because she was afraid this lady was going to do something else to her.

What crime do we have? None. There is no statute that

covers Witchcraft. We don't need one. What we need is education.

[Jim Bradley works in the intelligence division of the District of Columbia Metropolitan Police Department. Although the Cuban population of Washington, D.C. is relatively small, he has seen activity among *Santeros*. He is one of a handful of police officers who have direct knowledge of *Abaqua*, a small sect within the *Santeria* religion.]

DET. JIM BRADLEY: The Castro government doesn't recognize any religions except Catholicism, and they have banned all other religions with the exception of the *Abaqua* people. Castro does not want to deal with the *Abaqua* people. He doesn't want to offend their gods or their high priest, so he has stayed away from an area called Motanzas in central Cuba. That's also the name given to their sacrament, their ceremony, "*La Motanzas.*"

In 1978 in Havana, a legitimate play was put on titled *Abaqua*. It explained all the workings of the secret society. Within two weeks after this play was put on all the members of the cast—some twenty people—were killed.

You're born into the organization, the coconuts are thrown, the astrological criteria are known, and the priest selects who your saint will be. Once he makes his selection, you go through a cleansing ritual, sometimes two weeks of sexual abstinence, wearing of white garments up to the *Motanzas*, the day of the bloodletting. On that date you bring a white plate, white cup, white feather, white candle and the pieces of the coconut that the priest gave you. Depending upon who the priest believes in, that deity will usually be at the top and all the other six will be around. Santa Barbara, for example, on a white stallion, is really Chango.

The intelligence information I have picked up from here,

Miami and elsewhere is typical of how *Santeria* works. A high priest for instance—who is making money from his followers—may say that they aren't making enough. He directs his followers to commit certain acts in the name of Chango, Obalata . . . their particular god, because that's what the gods have transmitted to the high priest who then transmitted that to the followers. The followers would come and pray for protection against the police and rival gangs. *Santeria* gangs are involved in all kinds of felonies, just like traditional organized gangs. The only difference is the religious aspect.

Their methods are those not usually seen in the United States. They would rob a liquor store, for example, with ten people and five cars. I've never seen a robbery in Washington with five cars and ten people. They would completely take over everything in the store. Two people would sit outside, and if the police came they would ram the police cars. This was completely unconventional for crime in the United States prior to the time the Cubans arrived here. I'm not saying that all Cubans are criminals, but there are factions within this religious group that follow the guidelines that the priest lays down. A portion of the booty is delegated for the priest. It's a substantial amount, sometimes a third or a fourth. They do believe they will be protected by the gods. The priest sees to that.

Palo Mayombe is the dark side of *Santeria*. You will usually find a blackened skull with a candle coming out of the head. You will find a black cauldron filled with artifacts.

The most dangerous is the *Abaqua*, but they're also the most benevolent if you're a friend. In *Palo Mayombe* there's no benevolence at all. It's nothing but evil. The reason why I think *Abaqua* is the most dangerous is because they are so protective of themselves and the organization. *Abaqua* consider themselves righteous. They believe *Palo* is all bad.

[Francisco Rigores is a *Marielito* who is a high priest of the

Abaqua religion. He collects money from his followers for religious services which promise good health and protection from enemies. Some of his followers have been arrested for felonies including burglary, robbery, and weapons violations. Although he has acted without approval in the past, Rigores is currently negotiating with the D.C. government for permission to slaughter animals during his ceremonies in a manner acceptable to the community.]

FRANCISCO RIGORES: [translated from Spanish] I am a *Babalao* in the *Abaqua* religion. I was born in Motanzas in Cuba, and I was twelve years old when I entered the religion. I came to the United States in 1980 during the *Mariel* boatlift.

My job in Cuba was to guard the door during the *Abaqua* ceremonies that took place during the holy days like on December 4 and 17. [December 4 is the feast of Saint Barbara/Chango and December 17 is the feast of Saint Lazarus/Babaluaye.]

If you were not *varon* [literally, manly, but colloquially taken to mean not gay] you couldn't come in. A man can't touch a woman on the mouth then come in. If you do that you're not *varon*. Can't touch another man [sexually] then come into the place. In order to be in *Abaqua* you must be *varon*.

Castro tried to do away with the *Abaqua*, but he could not. He wanted to join it, but they wouldn't let him.

In order to be in *Abaqua* you must be *varon*. You must be a strong man, good father, good son, good friend. If somebody in *Abaqua* doesn't practice the religion correctly he can be removed.

I was in a Cuban prison for fifteen years, seven months. Castro took my carpenter shop, which my father handed down to me. I tried to retaliate against Castro, and he put me in prison.

If you want to join *Abaqua* you give in your name and

picture. Then it's taken around to everyone in the group. They do a background check, asking your mother and father, anyone who knows you. After they find that you are worthy, they have a conference and vote on you.

If you are accepted you will get your beads at the ceremony. [The colors of the beads are aligned with your particular Orisha.] One of the requirements is that you must not sleep with your wife for one week. You must wear different clothes. The family can wait outside during the ceremony.

At the *Motanzas*, there is water, coconuts, all kinds of fruits, flowers, and the animal. We cook it and give it away to the people after we are done with it. Each *Motanzas* has its own knife. The animal is slit up the middle lengthwise. I don't do anything with the blood. We clean it up. [Blood is often poured upon and drunk by participants during some *Santeros'* rituals.] There is music from the drums. The coconut will tell when to touch the conga drum . . . three days, five, whatever.

We do other things at the *Motanzas*. If you're going to have a son, put his name in a white plate, cover it with blood. Wash your hands with water from the river or rain. Never use water from the sink. This will ensure a healthy baby.

I must have a lot of power because people come to me. If people are sick they come to me. I've had power since I was twelve years old. I can help you get better if you are sick, but you must believe it. I would throw the coconuts. Anytime I ask anything, the coco will give me the answer. They will tell everything. You must believe in the coconuts. If the coco say I have to take you from the hospital, you have to go.

Palo Mayombe is not the same as *Abaqua*. It's two different things. The people now are not the same people who have practiced the religion before. It's almost like a different religion. Some people take the religion to cover something bad that they're doing. They practice the religion, but they don't do it the way they're supposed to be doing it. *Palo Mayombe* is not necessarily bad, but it depends upon how you use it.

There are people who practice bad things with the religion in Washington. In Maryland too. In Miami. Since I came to the United States I get mad when I run into people who say they are in the religion but are not.

The *Abaqua* never kills black animals. That's bad. Other people may kill a black rooster, black goat, black pigeons. I would never take a goat and put it to a woman's body. You never have good luck with anything black.

We bring animals from Frederick [a city outside of Washington, D.C.]. When we brought them here for the last *Motanzas* the police came. [The Humane Society seized the animals: goat, calf, pig, six doves, three chickens, three roosters and six quails. Rigores was to sacrifice them to celebrate his birthday and the feast day of Saint Francis/Orunla, his patron saint. The animals were to be part of a feast for friends and neighbors. Rigores was accused of mistreating the animals, mainly because they were tied tightly and kept in an unlit basement. The pig was in a small crate such that it couldn't move around.] I lost face in front of my people. I will kill animals in front of the White House if my animals are not returned to me. I will get a lot of people. I don't care if I go to jail.

A lot of people go to the Safeway [supermarket] and use the animals that are already dead. That's no good. I kill the animals and give it to the people. I want permission to kill animals any way the police say I can.

DET. JIM BRADLEY: The case of one Eloy Hernandez involves *Palo Mayombe*. When we first started after him, I thought he was a member of *Abaqua*. I knew he was a *Santero*, but I didn't know which sect. I knew he was involved in drugs [cocaine], and that gave us the go ahead. We had some informants make some controlled buys, and we executed a search warrant on his house.

He had a cauldron in the middle of the floor full of animal

bones, money, human bones, .45 caliber, crucifix, knife, neck-laces. He had what I call voodoo dolls, a red one, a white one, and black one. He had photos on the faces and pins in them. He had a snake in the cauldron, but you couldn't see it easily. I almost put my hand in there.

He had a statue of Saint Lazarus on crutches with dogs licking his wounds. He had beads on it. The bead's colors are aligned to the saint. [Saint Lazarus is syncretized to the god Babalu-aye, who is the patron saint of the sick and skin diseases. His colors are white and purple or white and light blue. Some believe that the late entertainer Desi Arnaz was praying to this god during his singing of "Babalu" while playing his conga drum.]

I had asked a Hispanic police officer to translate for me. I took the beads off the neck of Saint Lazarus and was playing with them. The officer dropped to his knees, at which time the priest knew that he had him. The priest said something to him in Spanish, and the officer turned to me and said, "I can't do the job; get someone else." I said, "You got to stay here and help." He said, "I've got an aunt back home, and the priest will put a spell on her, and she'll die." I said, "You're a police officer. Do you really believe this man could do this?" He said, "He already told me he would."

It was the first time I saw someone who was intelligent being commanded by an . . . an idiot. It was unbelievable. Once he dropped to his knees it was all over for the officer.

Hernandez did two years. He's now on parole.

[Roberto Rodriguez is the pseudonym of an undercover narcotics investigator in Miami.]

DET. ROBERTO RODRIGUEZ: The drug scene is changing almost daily in Miami. Now we're seeing new drug dealers from Colombia who are more ruthless than any others I've seen, and I've been on the force for almost ten years, three with narcotics. They are very heavily armed—Uzis, you name it.

We'll find dead bodies of dealers who were killed as part of a drug deal, and they were killed as part of a *Santeria* sacrifice. All the indicators are there. Sometimes we find small animals, chickens, ducks, whatever, along with the deceased that were sacrificed first.

These guys will wear necklaces with the color of their Orishas to protect them from the police. They sprinkle powders to keep away the law. One time we showed up late to a drug buy. Everyone was gone but we found dead animals that were sacrificed to ensure that the deal would go all right. This mixing of religion and crime is very dangerous. It gives these guys the feeling that they can't be touched, that they're somehow protected, like they were Superman. It makes them that much more wild and reckless and dangerous.

[P. J. Lawton is a detective with the youth and family services division of the Pima County Sheriff in Tucson. Several thousand *Marielitos* flocked to his area of Arizona after the 1980 boatlift. Within a few months, his department arrested 250 of them. Now that many are beginning to trickle out of prison, he is seeing an upsurge in crimes related to *Santeria*.

Police working with these criminals noticed unique tattoos, which some claim show the kind of crime they engage in. Other police believe the tattoos are unreliable as indicators. Both sides have their proponents. See chart on page 269.]

DET. P. J. LAWTON: When the *Marielitos* hit, Tucson got an extra large helping, because we already had a fairly large Cuban community. The Catholic services sponsored a bunch of them. They started doing bizarre stuff: murders, drugs, burglaries. At the time, I was working burglary and my sergeant gave me the assignment of figuring out who this group was and how to target them.

A Hispanic officer and I started picking them up, interviewing them and photographing tattoos. Eventually we got into the *Santeria* part of it because they were all claiming that they had been religiously persecuted in Cuba and things like that.

I've gotten different explanations on the hand tattoos. I don't really know what to believe. When they first started cropping up, that's what everyone started concentrating on. We thought if you had one symbol it meant "I'm into drugs" or another symbol means "I've killed somebody." If it's such and such a way it means "I believe in such and such a god."

I think what's happened is that there's been a blurring of crime and belief. They use their belief so much to justify their crimes that it ceases to be a difference between the crime and religion.

If they have *Santerian* beliefs, by knowing their patron saint you can pretty much figure out their type of crime. If they're a believer in Oggun, the god of warriors, metals and weapons, that translates to guns and knives. That means they're usually into violent stuff, assaults, murders.

If their patron saint is Oshun [controls gold, money, makes marriages] then they're less into violent stuff. I mean, they're all violent because they've been raised in the prison system of Cuba, but they are more into property crimes and drugs. It's not a hard and fast rule. I wouldn't testify to it, but the tattoos are an indicator.

DET. JIM BRADLEY: I don't put any stock in the tattoos. To believe that the tattoos meant such precise things would be impossible for me to believe because the whole religion is so unstructured. Why would they get structured when it came to putting dots on their hands?

DET. CLEO WILSON: As far as *Santeria* is concerned, only in the past year or year-and-a-half have we seen any signs of it here in Denver. We've found some symbolism and curse altars in empty lots, but haven't run into actual crimes in Denver. We haven't been asked to consult on any cases.

However, *Brujeria* is very extensive here because we have such a large Mexican community. The botanicas have things like mom's old remedies, and it's passed down from generation to generation, from *Bruja* to *Bruja*. It's also passed down to the rest of the Hispanic community. I would say that the majority of the Hispanics in Denver are aware of all the botanicas, and somebody knows the remedy for . . . whatever.

[In Spanish, *Bruja* means witch, and *Brujeria* literally means Witchcraft. Although some people call *Brujeria* the black side of *Santeria*, that is not technically correct. *Brujeria* comes from the Aztec pagan religion mingled with Catholicism, and has much in common with European Witchcraft. It is mainly concerned with folk magic, with an emphasis on herbal medicines, tarot card readings, astrology, and spells, and the main deity is female—in this case Our Lady of Guadalupe. Also, like other forms of Witchcraft, *Brujeria* can be benevolent or evil.

The origins of *Brujeria* are disputed. According to Spanish legends, the Blessed Virgin appeared to an Indian convert in 1531 and said that she wanted a mission built on the spot where he stood. The villagers claimed to see visions of a brown-skinned Madonna; the missionaries took that as a sign that the mission should indeed be built, and they called it Our Lady of Guadalupe.

Current day *Brujas* tell a different story. They say that long before the Spanish conquered their people, the Aztecs had prayed on that site to their own goddess, Tontantzin. As the cult of Guadalupe grew, the Spanish baptized Tontantzin and encouraged the Indians to exalt her. In doing so, they perpetuated the pagan worship of Tontantzin but insisted that the converted Indians call her Nuestra Senora de Guadalupe. Not unlike the syncretization of the *Santeria* gods and the Catholic saints, the *Brujas* continued the worship of their goddess.

Many Aztecs saw similarities between their old religion and Catholicism, which made the keeping of their own beliefs easier. For example, the Aztec had an afterlife for those with bad souls known as *Mictlan* which appeared to them very much like the Catholic version of hell. Also, because the act of human sacrifices was the province of males, the *Brujas* didn't flinch when the Catholics prohibited females from saying High Mass. The *Brujas* didn't admit men to some of their ceremonies either. During ceremonies, the *Brujas* used incense as did the priests.

As Mexicans moved to the United States, *Brujeria* continued to exist. In fact, it tended to pick up ideas from *Santeria* and Voodoo—one reason why law enforcement officials and others tend to think of Hispanic magick as all being the same.]

I am from a Hispanic family. I'm Mexican, and I know from my mom talking to me about the people who lived in the little town where she and my dad came from [Gardner, Colorado], who the *Bruja* was and what her powers were. Let me give you a story. These are stories that I was brought up on.

There was a story about the *Bruja* who was Maggie. That was the name of the *Bruja* in the town when my mother was growing up. She had the ability to make fire. There was a girl in the town who people felt was promiscuous. They watched the girl go to the dance. When she got to the dance she danced with this very handsome man. When they looked down they saw cloven hooves and a tail hanging down. Everybody was afraid. They knew she was dancing with the Devil.

They went to talk to the *Bruja* about it, and she said that she had told the priest that this thing was going to be at the dance and who it was going to dance with. It was because of her promiscuity that she had been chosen. The girl has a grand time, but when it comes time for the dance to end, he leaves, without warning, and she runs after him. She sees a ball of fire, hopping up the road, and he disappears. It was indeed the Devil.

Another story is about a man who had been unfaithful to his wife. In addition, he had beaten his wife and child. One night he went to meet his love and encountered a ghost. The ghost told him that he was "at that place of crossing over," and his decision at that time would determine his destiny. The man pooh-poohed it and continued on to his lady friend's house. When he got there, she was dead, and the same ghost was there. The man was tried and convicted of her murder.

Coming from this background of legends and folklore, I assumed everyone knew about *Brujeria*. I thought everyone knew that if you had an abscessed tooth you took part of the abscess, swabbed it with a leaf and buried it. And if you had a wart you rubbed it with a dishrag and buried it. Burying things is symbolic of death.

Witchcraft goes back forever, to Paganism. You see elements of Witchcraft in Satanism, *Brujeria* and *Santeria*.

Where all these religions go bad is when people aren't satisfied to live within the environment they have created. It's not enough to have power over themselves. They want to control the heavens and each other. As the need for more power grows, occult crime increases. It attracts people who aren't satisfied; they want more power. The more powerful you are, the more people you have power over, and the more powerful you become in turn.

But the more you study occult crimes the more you realize that this behavior isn't exclusive to non-traditional religions. It's true of all religions, Satanism, *Brujeria*, *Santeria*, even Catholicism; look at the Inquisition. What it comes down to, in the end, is being a sick human being.

CHAPTER EIGHT:

THE RITUALS

All occult rituals revolve around one theme: summoning of supernatural power that can then be used to effect a change. Except under controlled circumstances, occult groups will not allow outsiders to view their rituals. When they do, outsiders don't see a real working but one that has been contrived for the outsider. By their very nature, workings can't be shown to those who aren't members or believers. To do so would sap the strength of the working and render it impotent.

Most rituals or ceremonies employed by occult groups follow a similar vein, but they differ from group to group and even among people within the same group.

FEATHER: During our ritual we raise power, and we send that power to do whatever it is we want it to do. If someone is sick and they have asked for our help then we will do a healing.

At one time I didn't have a mate. I wrote on a piece of parchment that I wanted a companion. I didn't name anyone, because that wouldn't be fair. It would be practicing magick on someone else without their consent. I asked for a companion who would be good to me, help me financially, help me mentally, be my friend, share my life. I used red ink because that color stands for affairs of the heart. We put it in the fire so the smoke would go to the "higher-up."

It worked. I got a call out of the blue from a guy I knew when I was sixteen years old. He's thirty-seven, never been married. It will take some time, but I think we're going to get together. I'm happy about that.

[Many occult groups use a circle. For some groups it offers protection from unruly spirits; for others it is a place into which power is conjured.]

MARGOT ADLER: The circle is a protective space where you can let down your guard. There's a lot of womb symbolism. Who knows what Gerald Gardner was thinking when he made it nine feet? It may have been nine months gestation; the circle is the womb. The circle is a place of no beginning and no end. The main thing is that the circle is a way of delineating sacred space. In Witchcraft terminology, it's between the worlds and therefore doesn't concern the worlds. You're free to let down your psychic guard and enter the dream reality, an altered state of consciousness, and feel safe.

DET. SANDI GALLANT: I always take what occultists tell me with a grain of salt. You never know if what they're telling you is the truth, because they always want to paint a better picture than what may really be going on.

From what I've heard and researched, many of the groups are concerned when they call upon the evil spirits that they may become unruly. They will use the circle as an area for protection for themselves. They won't conjure the demons into that area but into an area approximately two feet away which may be a triangle or some other shape. Usually the spirit comes down and becomes one of the people in the room. I would assume that person isn't allowed into the area of protection but is outside of it. It's important that the participants know that the spirit or demon has been cast out before they leave the area of protection.

All this depends upon the group. Some don't believe they need the protection of a circle while others, especially new groups that may not feel comfortable with the powers that they may hold, will not conjure power into the circle.

Some of the traditional groups think that's silly. For one thing, you don't go to lesser demons and, second, what is there to protect yourself from anyway?

DR. MICHAEL AQUINO [*The Crystal Tablet of Set*]: No protective circles or pentacles on the floor or anywhere else are necessary. Since the Black Magickian is at one with the Powers of Darkness, he needs no protection from them. Nor, it may be said, are circles or pentacles the slightest deterrent to these Powers save in the subjective universe of a superstitious white magickian.

[Nolan Waters is the pseudonym of a Satanist in the New York City area. He asked that his name not be used for fear of retaliation from his employer who does not know his religious affiliation. Waters is a department administrator for a municipal government. He is in his early forties.]

NOLAN WATERS: My group follows a ritual based loosely on what's found in *The Satanic Bible*. We combine it with rituals that we found in ancient books. As we progressed, we began to modify more and more until we found something that worked best for us. We're still experimenting. We write down our rituals, and if they work we use them again. If not, they are modified. Magick is experimental.

First we all dress in our robes. We use black for most rituals, but we also use red for sex magick. The same goes for candles that we light. We use black or red. Sometimes we use white, but not very often. Candles provide an eerie illumination, just right for a working.

We built our own altar out of wood, and we usually use one of our female members on top of it as the actual altar.

She is nude. The significance of her is that she represents carnal power and lust. Satan represents indulgence, as you know.

Our chamber is painted matte black, and it is only illuminated by the candles. In the middle we have a pit that we fill with wood and have a pretty good flame going before we start. [The rituals are held at a member's house, but in the summer they are often held outside in isolated areas of public parks.]

The first thing we do is ring the bell. It's a regular bell like you'd find in an old time school house. The bell lets everyone know that we've begun. It acts as a break between the world we came from and the world we will be entering.

Next we have the chalice. I drink from it first, because I'm the high priest. Usually it contains wine, but sometimes fruit juice. It depends upon the kind of working we're doing.

Sometimes, if the working is going to be dangerous, I don't want to be impaired, even by a little wine. Drugs are a bone of contention. Some members have to smoke a little pot to get relaxed enough to do the ceremonies, to release their energy. I don't discourage it. Other members use cocaine because they believe it heightens their senses and gets them piqued to accept the spirits.

Next we call upon Satan. I can't tell you exactly what we say because the words are sacred to our group. It's a mixture of many different invocations that have been used over the centuries. Basically, we ask the Prince of Darkness or sometimes lesser demons to come into our sanctuary. Once we feel the power around us—it can take a while or sometimes it doesn't happen at all—we know that Satan is here.

As the priest, I tell Satan what we want. Sometimes it's more money, a better job, sometimes it's revenge. It's for anyone in the group with a desire. Sometimes we ask for more than one thing, but we try to find things that are compatible. For instance, we may decide that on this certain night we're only going to do destructive magick. The group will save up its demands for that night that concern hurting someone else. We would never hurt anyone within the group. But we couldn't give a shit about someone outside. There are always thirteen of us present.

We demand things in two ways: one is that we ask for it verbally, but that doesn't have as much power as when we write it on parchment, place it on the end of the sword and burn it in the pit. The smoke mixes with spirits in the air. After each piece is burned we usually say "Hail Satan!" plus any lesser demons that are the favorite of anyone in the group at that time. Sometimes a ritual can take several hours. Usually we do them on a Friday night. When it is over we all say together: "So it is done."

People talk a lot about Satanists killing animals and so forth. I'm sure some of them do. We don't need to do that. We can get enough power without it. I do know of groups that do. We partake in sex magick. I don't think many people would approve of that. We find it increases the group's power. I can't get into the details of what that's about because some of it is illegal.

DET. PAT METOYER: I got introduced to a lady whose name was Dia, from the Church of Satan in Van Nuys. I went to a ritual where a six-week-old baby was baptized into the Church of Satan. They tried to find one [a ritual] to show me that Satanism was a real religion. They came up with the baptism. They wouldn't let me attend any other meetings that they had.

It started at midnight. I got there; it was at a small home. One of the bedrooms had been converted into a sacristy. The walls, ceiling and floor were in matte black. Iridescent paint had been splattered on the ceiling and walls. Even if you put an eight-thousand-watt bulb in that room it would have been dark. There was a huge mural of Satan on the wall. It was a person with human features, red, with horns. There was an altar made of wood, painted matte black. There was *The Satanic Bible*, black and white candles, a bell and a chalice. They told me not to touch the altar because I was unclean.

The north wall had effigies of persons who had turned on the organization or who had been brought to the group's attention by one of the members. There was someone's supposed liver in wax with pins in it.

The only part that got to me initially was that they insisted on taking my photograph. No picture, no come in. So they took my picture. I smiled for them, really no big deal. The reason they wanted my picture was in the event I turn on them at some point they can use that in lieu of fingernail clippings or something else.

Then they tried to frighten me by saying, "In the past we've had people who didn't believe us so we took their photograph and put it in the freezer, and they would get cold chills. Then we would put it in the oven, and they would get hot flashes." I said "Okay" to all this bullshit.

Then Dia said, "I don't think you believe us." I said, "That's true. I don't." She says, "If my aura were to attack you would that make you a believer?" I said, "No, it wouldn't." She said, "Turn your back to me, and you will feel my power." I turned around and faced the wall. My back was to her. She said, "Can you feel anything?"

"No."

"How about now?"

"No."

"How about now?"

"No."

"Now I'm sure you can feel something." She was getting frustrated, and I could tell she was getting frustrated. The people there were getting a little antsy. So I said, "Ah yes, I can feel it," even though I didn't.

She said, "Thank you. You have a little stronger will than

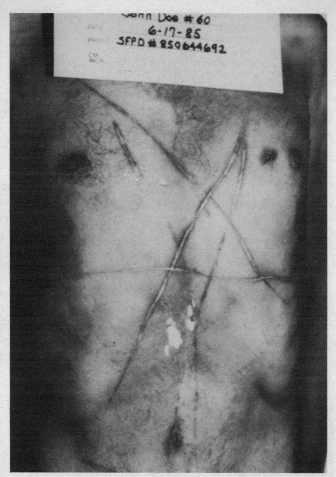

This is the body of an unidentified man, known only as John Doe #60, who was killed during a Satanic ritual in San Francisco in June 1985. His killer, Clifford St. Joseph, was found guilty of first-degree murder on March 14, 1988 (see chapter 5).

A pentagram had been carved in the victim's chest and his body had partially been drained of blood during the ritual. Candle-wax drippings were found in his right eye. During the trial's closing arguments, Prosecutor Paul Cummings described the proceedings as a "voyage into an underworld we don't want to admit exists in our society." *Courtesy San Francisco Police Department*

This graveyard in Mt. Airy, Maryland, was desecrated in October 1986 by a group of five youths aged 16–18 who engaged in Satanic worship. The leader of the group, an 18-year-old, was convicted of 106 counts of vandalism and stealing the remains of a 6-week-old girl during the rampage. He was sentenced to 18 months. The others were given lesser sentences. About 60 gravestones were overturned and inverted crosses were placed by some graves as homage to the Devil. *Courtesy Tim Boyle, Maryland National Capital Park Police*

This decapitated deer was found near a school building in Wheaton, Maryland. An inverted cross was spray-painted on the carcass, and investigators found occult symbols on the building's walls. The condition of the dead animal was consistent with that of animals often used in occult sacrifices. No arrests were made. *Courtesy Tim Boyle, Maryland National Capital Park Police*

Unless a law enforcement officer actually witnesses an occult ritual, he cannot say for certain that a site had been used for such an activity. However, physical evidence left behind offers good indication that occult activity had occurred.

This site was found in a playground in San Francisco's Duboce Park. Seen in this night photo is a hexagram within a circle and a candle in the center. In occult rituals "magic circles" are used as an area into which supernatural power is conjured. *Courtesy San Francisco Police Department*

This site was discovered in Potomac, Maryland, in a wooded area. An inverted cross made of twigs was placed atop a makeshift plywood structure, Graffiti can be seen in the background. A brazier was found nearby. *Courtesy Tim Boyle, Maryland National Capital Park Police*

This unusual site was found in southern California. The "magic circle" was composed of pine leaves. Inside is a cross and a raised triangle of dirt. *Courtesy Judy Hanson*

This site was found in Oakland County, Michigan, north of Detroit, in a clearing in the woods. You can see an altar *(middle)* and a throne *(right side)*. This area was discovered by a police officer who had attended a seminar on occult crime. *Courtesy Dale Griffis*

Because sexually abused children often can't talk openly about what happened, therapists sometimes ask them to draw pictures. These drawings were done by an eight-year-old girl, pseudonymously named Rhonda (see chapter 12), who was sexually abused in a ritualistic manner. She described animal and human sacrifices, people standing in circles and chanting prayers to Satan.

Rhonda's drawings show a dagger, flags, and what appears to be a swastika. She told investigators that adults in the group looked at a picture of a man with a mustache and said "hail." Some black magic groups have studied the Nazi's obsession with the occult and adopted some of the Third Reich's practices in their own ceremonies.

This shows a man carrying a baby into the room where Rhonda said the ritual took place. She told investigators that the baby's legs were placed in a fire before being sacrificed.

Rhonda drew two children lying on an altar and herself kneeling in front. She told investigators that her father forced her to stab a baby—whose legs were first placed in the fire *(above right*—note name "daddy")—while he held her hands around a dagger. When asked what she saw, she responded: "I saw worms come out." Investigators, unsure what she meant about "worms," suggest it could mean intestines.

Rhonda wrote this note describing her feelings about her mother and father.

Although most practitioners of Santeria ("worship of the saints") are law-abiding, remnants and paraphernalia used in the form of Hispanic witchcraft are often found at crime scenes.

Although Santeros are not Devil worshipers, because of their Catholic underpinning, some may believe in the Christian concept of Satan. This drawing, on the door of a room where rituals take place, is the mark of the Devil. It is a crucifix with a snake wrapped around it. *Courtesy Jim Bradley, D.C. Metropolitan Police Dept.*

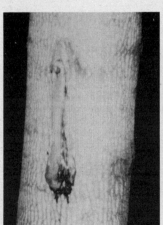

This cow tongue was found nailed to a tree in Montgomery County, Maryland (see chapter 7). Beneath the tree was a full set of man's clothing, seven coins (representing the seven Santeria gods or Orishas), a Cuban cigar, and a dead bird. Police believe the tongue was a warning to those involved in a nearby Cuban-run drug ring not to talk to authorities about their activities. *Courtesy Tim Boyle, Maryland National Capital Park Police*

Santeros will use various items in their ceremonies depending upon which Orisha is being worshiped. Here you see a picture of Jesus Christ, candles, and pieces of iron on a white plate as an offering to the god Eleggua. This deity also likes seashells (on the white plate under the picture) and rum (in the goblet in the foreground). *Courtesy Jim Bradley, D.C. Metropolitan Police Dept.*

Animal sacrifices are prevalent in Santeria practices. Here a ram's head is placed on a white plate. On the plate next to it are colored necklaces atop a sacrificed fowl. Each Orisha has his own set of colors, which are displayed in the necklaces worn by adherents. *Courtesy Jim Bradley, D.C. Metropolitan Police Dept.*

This is the partially decomposed head of Leroy Carter (see chapter 2), whose decapitated body was found exactly 42 days before in San Francisco's Golden Gate Park in 1981. The headless body was discovered with a chicken feather stuffed in the neck and corn kernels (an appeasement to an Orisha) nearby. Police investigators believe the head—which appeared close to the site where the body was found—may have been used in a Santeria ritual in which it was buried for 21 days and then used to generate supernatural power during another 21-day period. The homicide has not been solved. *Courtesy San Francisco Police Department*

Capt. Dale Griffis (retired),
Tiffin, Ohio, Police Department
Photo by Ken Egbert

Det. Sandi Gallant,
Intelligence Division,
San Francisco Police Department
*Courtesy San Francisco
Police Department*

Det. Bill Wickersham,
Denver Police Department
*Photo by Det. John Ballegeer,
Denver P.D.*

Det. Cleo Wilson,
Denver Police Department
*Photo by Det. John Ballegeer,
Denver P.D.*

I thought," as if I was trying to play some mental head game with her.

You have to equate that with you going to my church, St. John's, and during the course of the mass you get up laughing or screaming. The parishioners are not going to take very kindly to that. It's inappropriate behavior. I felt that my action of not feeling her power was inappropriate to their church, so I said I did. They performed the baptism which seemed like a lot of mumbo jumbo.

THE SATANIC "BAPTISM"
Children's Ceremony
[from *The Satanic Rituals*]

Opening statement:
"In the name of Satan, Lucifer, Belial, Leviathan and all the demons, named and nameless, walkers in the velvet darkness, harken to us, O dim and shadowy things, wraith-like, twisted, half-seen creatures, glimpsed beyond the foggy veil of time and spaceless night. Draw near, attend us on this night of fledgling sovereignty. Welcome a new and worthy brother, creature of exquisite magic light. Join us in our welcome. With us say: welcome to you, child of joy, sweet passion's son, product of the dark and musk filled night, ecstasy's delight. Welcome to you, sorcerer most natural and true magickian. Your tiny hands have strength to pull the crumbling vaults of spurious heavens down and from their shards erect a monument to your own sweet indulgence. Your honesty entitles you to well deserved dominion o'er a world filled with frightened, cowering men.

DET. PAT METOYER: At the end they had this meeting where they sit around and talk about what Satan had done for them. People would tell what happened to them since the last meeting. They would tell about the demands they had made to Satan. You never ask Satan, you demand. In other religions you make a petition, you ask for something. Here you demand it. That's what they say they like about Satanism. You never get on your knees. You say, Satan, give me this!

JUDY HANSON: Satan has been granted power over the earth, according to the Old Testament. Therefore they will pay him homage because he is closer to them than God up in heaven. They are highly religious people. Their rituals are often precise and the people are devout.

GWYN GWYNALLEN: What people sometimes forget when they look at Witchcraft or Satanic ceremonies is that the Catholic Mass is a spiritual ceremony, too. By praying and chanting, the congregation and priest are bringing into the church the spirit of Christ. You have the drinking of wine which symbolizes the blood of Christ and the host which symbolizes taking his flesh.

CAPT. DALE GRIFFIS: The use of blood in Satanic rituals is very important. According to the beliefs, blood contains the life force. If you have it, you have power. That's why they drink it in their rituals and pour it over themselves.

So is sacrificing people. When you sacrifice someone, for the instant just before they die, they supposedly emit their life energy. That power, Satanists believe, can be harnessed for their use. They believe babies are best because babies are pure; they haven't sinned or been corrupted yet. They possess a higher power than adults. When you sacrifice a baby, you get greater power than if you sacrificed an adult. One of the most prized possessions of a Satanist is a candle made from the fat of an unbaptized baby.

DET. SANDI GALLANT: Some Satanists believe that with specific body parts they can use the power contained therein. The head may contain the spirit, and the heart may contain the soul. These are things that would allow them to be in control. It's been said they like to have a finger of the left hand. I don't know exactly why the finger. I understand about the left and right paths, but why the finger? Who knows?

DEPUTY PROBATION OFFICER DARLYNE PETTINICCHIO: You want to hear the stories the kids tell me about rituals? This one kid told me about something that happened to her when she was thirteen years old. She's fifteen now. Her parents were divorced. Neither one is really interested in the kid. The mother is involved in some lesbian relationship, and the kid is always running off. From her house, she would look down the hill and see a bunch of kids. They looked like they were always having fun. So, she ended up running away and meeting up with them.

They had a little cult. The cults I deal with are not formal Satanic cults. They're kids who get together, take a little from this book and that book, and add a little of their own. They get a nineteen-year-old to be the high priest, and they dabble. In this instance they had a twenty-one-year-old high priest.

She said one night they brought in three kids who were loaded, and they were going to have a ritual. She said that she was always loaded when she was with this group. She couldn't stand to do it otherwise. I asked how loaded they were. I was trying to get an idea. She said they had to carry them in.

They brought them in and apparently these three had ripped off the little Satanists in a dope deal. They started the ritual; they rang the bell, they did an invocation to Satan. Then they went out to the hills—she drew me a map—where there was a chain and some trees. They had cans of gasoline, and they did the ritual and brought one guy out and threw him in the middle. They all had candles, and the high priest threw the candle on him and he was torched like that. The girl said he wasn't that loaded that he wasn't screaming and yelling. They just let him burn.

She said they brought another kid out, a girl, and one of the boys was feeling her up, she got sick and left. She said, "I knew the same thing was going to happen to me."

I tried to get the LASO [Los Angeles Sheriff's Office] to talk to the kid. Two officers were willing to talk to her, but the public defender stepped in and said no. They would not let her talk. They represented her in another case, and they were afraid that they were going to press charges on her. That wasn't the case, but they wouldn't believe it. The police weren't going to file charges, they just wanted the information. [The incident is still under investigation, and those involved would not discuss it.]

I think they really stifled her growth by not letting her talk about it. She needs to deal with this. That's what really concerned me. I know they were trying to protect her rights, but I think part of her right is the right to get rid of that.

CHAPTER NINE:

THE PHYSICAL
EVIDENCE

Satanic cults are careful about calling attention to themselves. Law enforcement officials and others have come upon physical evidence of their activities, however. The most commonly found evidence is mutilated animals, ritual sites, and robbed graves.

The Animals

During the 1970s, the midwest was hit by an epidemic of animal mutilations. States were reporting incidents by the hundreds, and the news media were teeming with stories. Usually the victims were dairy cows, but horses and beef cattle were also found dismembered. The theories flew; everything from UFOs to natural predators such as wolves, to pranksters doing it just to drive the local sheriff crazy. Part of the mystery was that in many cases footprints of the perpetrators were never found. In other cases, the animals were found miles from where they belonged.

In retrospect, some things are clear. The animals were killed and mutilated in a deliberate and skillful manner. Judging by what was done to the animals—what body parts were taken, the fact that blood was drained—Satanic cults may have played a role.

Although it rarely makes the news anymore, mutilations continue today in all areas of the country.

CAPT. DALE GRIFFIS: I get a lot of calls about animal mutilations, probably because I'm in the midwest. There was a time when it seemed that it was going on all over the midwest. I got one call from a farmer in Indiana, not too far from Elkhart. He lost five head of cattle; someone had gone in and cut the vaginas out. He had one cow left, and he was going to sit up all night with a shotgun. He was going to get those bastards.

Why would someone cut out the sex organs? In Satanic religion, the sex organs are supposed to contain power. Satanism is a religion based on hedonism and the belief that the release of sexual energy is one way for you to reach a higher consciousness. You want anything that can add power to your rituals. By taking the sexual organs of an animal, you have some of that energy for your use.

I talked to the law enforcement people involved, told them what to look for, and they went back and started to look for Satanic paraphernalia at the scene. They were able to build up indicators that there was a traditional occult group in the area. As it turned out, the animal mutilations occurred a couple of days before an occult holiday.

From some of the people I've talked to, and autopsy reports that I've seen of animals that appear to have been used for rituals, occultists will stun the animal on his back with an electric probe. Then they will spray freon on the animal's throat. The animal is living, but he's not living, if you know what I mean. The heart's still pumping, and they will use an embalming tool to get the blood out. It's fast and efficient. Hell, the farmer heard the animal whine, and he was there within five minutes.

I still get calls all the time. It's become almost an everyday thing. I can't say that every call I get about an animal mutilation is Satanic in nature—most incidents remain unsolved or I don't hear back from the people I've consulted—but the evidence would lead you to think that the only reason for the mutilation is for an occult ritual of some kind.

[Eyewitnesses have been able to explain the mysteries involved in some mutilations.]

MEMO
TO: SHERIFF CARL STOBAUGH
Subject: Animal Mutilations
On 8-14-79 Sheriff Gus Anglin (Van Buren Co.) Arkansas, chief investigator, Jerry Bradley (Faulkner Co.), Sgt. King (ASP), and this officer interviewed a 23-year-old W/F whose identity must be kept confidential in reference to the recent cattle mutilations in this area. The young lady related the following story to us.

That for five years she was a higher echelon member of a Satanic worshipping cult which was headquartered in Tulsa, Oklahoma. During her five years there she was involved numerous times in trips to outlying remote areas where cattle were killed and the blood drawn out by use of an old embalming machine, which they had converted to battery power. They also removed the cow's eyes, tongue, sex organs and sometimes the udder.

She related the cult she belonged to was quite wealthy and had a helicopter and several van type trucks which were used in obtaining the organs and blood needed from the cows to be used in their rituals. She also stated that doctors, lawyers, veterinarians and other prominent persons belonged to this cult and were all taught by doctors and vets how to precisely cut the parts needed and exactly where to stick the needle to draw out the blood.

She stated the blood was put into gallon jugs and kept cool for baptizing new cult members. They were baptized in the same manner in which most churches do except the baptismal vat would be filled with blood which had been extracted from the animals. The eyes taken were boiled and eaten by the cult members at rituals. The sex organs were used in the rituals, also, because the cult believes in free sex to everyone.

When using the helicopter they sometimes picked up the cow by using a home made belt type sling and one man would go down and fasten it around the cow, and they would move it and drop it further down from where the mutilations occurred. This would account for there not being any footprints or tire tracks.

When using the van trucks they would also have a telescoping lift which she stated was about 200 feet long mounted outside the truck and would use that to extend a man out to the cow, and he would mutilate it from a board platform on the end of the boom and would never touch the ground.

She stated that they love the publicity that surrounds the mutilations, and as long as the publicity is in one area they will keep returning because they like to baffle law enforcement.

She stated that they would repeatedly go back to one farm if there were a number of roads coming into the area which would be accessible for a quick get away route. If not, they usually hit one time and then move on to another location. They sometimes do three or four cows a night.

The cult usually prefers the dairy cattle but will mutilate any type of cow when no dairy herds are easily found. They will also mutilate cattle which have died if they are still fresh and haven't started to deteriorate. They have mutilated bulls, horses, and dogs to get blood for their rituals.

She left the cult about a year ago because one couple sacrificed their 15-month-old baby. They placed the little girl on a table at one of the rituals and placed oil on her body and cut her up with a large knife to prove their love for Satan. She said that after seeing this she realized that the cult was not for love and left. She was beaten by some cult members a few months later who located her and was apparently left for dead.

She has agreed to cooperate in any way she can as long as her identity is kept a secret, because she fears for her life.

Ray Coffin
Chief Investigator
* * *

The Sites

Finding an actual site used in Satanic rituals is not easy. First, sites are well hidden in out-of-the-way places. Second, if Satanists believe they have been discovered they will destroy the site and move to another area. This is especially true of buildings that have been used for rituals. Some Satanists will move their sites on a regular basis. Third, many of the more prosperous Satanic cults ensure that their actions will not be detected by using private lands owned by a member.

Many law enforcement agencies don't report Satanic sites in such a way that the information can be accumulated. If the site is in a park, for instance, it may be recorded as "vandalism" or "destruction of public property." Also, because not all police officers know what a site looks like, they may simply describe it as an area where people congregate.

OFFICER TIM BOYLE: We run across a great number of sites because we patrol the parks. The most impressive site we've run across was in 1985 off Little Falls Parkway [Montgomery County, Maryland]. One of our officers stumbled upon it. Very often our officers get out and walk around. They're encouraged to do that. He saw warning signs and walked in a little farther and found this circled area where the trees had been cut out. He just stopped there. He didn't want to deal with it. We tell our officers now, if you don't want to deal with it, you don't have to. Cordon off the area like a crime scene, and call someone who can deal with it.

We don't want to interfere with any police officer's religious beliefs, but you don't screw up a crime scene because of your beliefs.

We don't believe this area was compromised. I asked the officer if he checked the ashes and he said, "I got the hell out of there." He got back and filed his report.

EXCERPT OF REPORT RD#1417-14-1285
MARYLAND NATIONAL CAPITAL PARK POLICE
MONTGOMERY COUNTY DIVISION
TUES. 12-31-85, 1013 HOURS
CRIME: VANDALISM

On 12-31-85 at about 1013 hours Lewis on routine patrol observed a worn foot path leading up a steep hill from the B&O railroad tracks (see area map). At the top of the hill, Lewis observed where suspect(s) unknown had cut about twenty sapling trees, value $10 each ($200 total) dug a pit about five feet by five feet by four feet, covered the pit with wood and metal and had spray painted numerous messages and warning. Some of the messages were "beware" "Go Back" "You're next" "DEATH 2 YOU"

"BURN IN HELL" "SAC RELM RULES." [Investigators don't know what this phrase means.] There were numerous references to demonic and satanic matters such as "LUCIFER," "666," inverted crucifixes and a five pointed star in a circle. There is also indication of burning and cages for animals.

Lewis left the scene as it was; there was evidence of suspect(s) being there within a few days (Jan. issue of Open University catalog) and no maintenance order has yet been submitted, pending development of suspect(s).

OFFICER TIM BOYLE: We went down there and investigated it ourselves. They had cleared the trees. They had two fire pits and warnings all along the outside to keep people away. There was a stone altar with candle wax on it, pentagrams and "666" written on it. It had a perfectly done circle, exactly nine feet across. It was done by the book. A lot of work had gone into it. There were cages that were the right size to hold small animals. There were nooses off the trees. [Nooses are often found at Satanic sites because they contribute to the macabre ambience. They are not necessarily used to hang anything.] It was a good way in the woods off some railroad tracks.

It was two miles from Secretary of State Shultz's house in an affluent area of Montgomery County. There was a large public outcry. People wanted to know what was going on. People called on us for the answers, and quite frankly we didn't have all the answers.

At the time I said, "Gentlemen, we don't know what we're doing. I know we have something serious, but I don't know exactly what, so let's handle it like a regular crime scene." That's what we did. We dug it out; we used metal detectors.

We called some priests, but they didn't want to talk. They said to call the archdiocese, because they weren't permitted to talk about it.

We're very fortunate that we had a good administration. The chief is former U.S. Park Police. He worked in Washington, Boston, and New York. He was well traveled and understood that there was an upswing in this kind of crime. Although these aren't his exact words, he basically said that if we wanted to find out about it we should get our ass in gear and find out about it. We were very fortunate that we had him. Our previous chief would have said screw it. I don't want to hear about that devil shit.

There was evidence that people had been there recently, but we didn't find any trace of bones, human or otherwise, in the pits. The site was fairly new.

We now hold classes on occult crimes. We tell our officers that we have information from agencies in other states that people have been murdered in these kinds of areas so don't screw it up. We tell our officers that when they're investigating a site, especially one that's being used, be careful of radio communications. They sometimes put guards on the outside of the site who are supposed to have powers to know when the police are coming. We call the power "Radio Shack scanner." We have special procedures for radio communications when handling these incidents.

We're not overwhelmed by Satanic activity, just like Montgomery County isn't overwhelmed with a lot of murders either, but you have to know how to investigate them.

We did finally work up a suspect who has since moved out of the area. We believe he's practicing his religion elsewhere.

DET. SANDI GALLANT: Just before I was to leave for the FBI academy, I got a call on Saturday night at home. It was some officers from Richmond station, which takes in some of Golden Gate Park. They had gotten a report of a woman screaming at Julius Kahn playground. It's a city park that sits on the edge of the Presidio. They went there, looked all around but didn't find anything. They saw a gardener's shed that had a light on, and they could hear music coming from inside. There was nobody inside, but they found a pentagram on the floor with a circle around it and another circle around that. There was also some foreign writing in the circle. There was nothing else that would have suggested anything occult except this circle that was obviously used for some workings.

They ended up making a report of a suspicious occurrence and my partner and I followed up and went and talked to the director of the playground. We thought he knew a little bit more than he was willing to tell us. He got us in contact with the gardener so we could take a look inside the shed. The gardener was extremely cooperative, kind of a hippie type guy which was rare for the eighties.

We never did find out what was going on there.

DET. CLEO WILSON: At our seminars, park rangers will often come up to us and tell us what they found. It has become so common for many of them that sometimes they don't even report it. You have to remember that park rangers are in a perfect position to see the results of Satanic activity. We had one ranger tell us about an opening in the woods where people were leaving just as he got there. There was a fire, candles all around and a pentagram in the dirt. They never did catch anybody, but they wondered what had gone on there. After our lecture, I think he understood more about what occurred.

DET. PAT METOYER: By the Pasadena Freeway there are drainage ditches that drain into the arroyo. If you walk there you'll see Satanic graffiti, evidence of red candle wax, white and black, and some sort of sacrificial offering evidence, the bones of some small animal of some kind. They may go out and buy a small white rat for all I know. They're probably involved in some kind of Satanic offerings. If I wanted to truly honor the devil where do you think I would go? I'd go some place that was slimy, that stinks like hell, that was secretive. Where better could I go than some drainage ditch.

[Ken Lawrence is the pseudonym of a police officer of an East Coast city. He works undercover.]

INVESTIGATOR KEN LAWRENCE: We picked up this kid for shoplifting, and he told us about a site where he and his friends would hold rituals. Rituals? I didn't know what he was talking about. He began telling us stories about worshiping the devil and so on, but my partner and I had no idea what he was talking about. We had heard something, not much, in police circles about occult crimes, and we contacted Dale Griffis and Sandi Gallant to find out what this was all about. We heard they were the ones to talk to about this. We got a crash course, and we had the kid take us to the site. He said it wasn't being used anymore.

As it turns out, he said his group never used the site, that it was a different group, but I didn't believe him. We walked about a quarter mile into the woods right off the main avenue and came to a clearing. It looked like there had once been a building there, because there was a large cement slab. It looked like a piece of a sidewalk, actually. It was a little overgrown, but we could see a pentagram inside a circle painted in white. It was the exact size—nine feet—that you're supposed to use.

There was a brick wall that was used as an altar. You could tell because there was candle wax all over the place. The pentagram was fading, and it was clear that it wasn't being used now. There were triangles near the pentagram.

It blew my mind; right here in the city—devil worshipers. My partner and I have been looking into it, but we've been keeping a low profile. We've continued talking to the kids. It's unbelievable the stuff they're into.

United States Department of Interior
National Park Service
CASE INCIDENT RECORD

Park Name: Golden Gate National Recreation Area
Location, Ft. Miley West
Reported by T. Lakeman
Case No. 003168, 04-12-80, 11 hrs. 00 min.
Nature of Incident: Unauthorized Camping
How Reported: Observation
Details,

I observed what appeared to be a place set up for devil worship in the open bunker area. The area had a figurine painted on the floor. Someone had also drilled holes in the ceiling and plugged them with wooden dowels. These dowels had ropes attached which appeared to be for restraining people. There were also numerous candles, athames and other artifacts. There is also bedding in the adjacent room.

[No further action was taken beyond securing and restoring the site.]

[Besides his work with *Santeria*, P. J. Lawton has followed closely occult activities atop Mount Lemmon, Arizona, and surrounding areas.]

DET. P. J. LAWTON: We've had some incidents on Mount Lemmon and also at Saguaro National Monument West. We've had some witches covens' meetings up there. We've seen other sites up there, mostly crude inverted crosses, fire pits. No sacrifices that we can attest to.

Saguaro National Monument West has an unusually thick section of cacti. There's two units, east and west. East costs money to get in and has more control. At West there's more access, and the local witches find it's a good place to have their ceremonies. Also, some native American groups have ceremonies there, too.

We had one site where we found cremated bones. According to our local pathologist, they looked like commercial cremation remains. These were human bones. The site corresponds to an offshoot religious spot. Like recently when we had the harmonic convergence where all the weirdos went to hold hands and chant, this site is near there. There was evidence of quite a few cremation remains so it might just be a convenient place for people to throw out Grandpa, but we really don't know.

Recently in the same area we found a rattlesnake talisman and white candle wax, so we don't know if we're dealing with a witch's site, a native American Indian site, or something darker.

Mount Lemmon is a prominent landmark. About a year ago we had a group of middle-teenagers from Catalina City just north of Tucson. There was a professor at the university who teaches religious studies, and he had built a full scale Sioux sweat lodge. They located that and thought it would be a good place to have their meetings. They ended up sacrificing a few goats and some chickens. I've interviewed all of them and only one would admit to it. The rest adamantly denied it, of course. They may have had an adult leader or advisor. I had some idea who it might have been, but I could never prove anything.

[Darrel Toellner is a deputy sheriff with the Carbon County Sheriff's Department in Rawlins, Wyoming.]

DEPUTY SHERIFF DARREL TOELLNER: One of our game wardens found the site. Those guys will go places that most of us would fear to tread, as they say. He found it, and gave us a call.

It's out in the Shirley Basin area way, way out in the country. There's nothing there. It's classified as high desert area, a lot of sagebrush. You can raise some cattle out there, but not a lot of it. It looked like somebody went to a lot of trouble to build a throne, maybe a chair. And a table. The throne was made of wood. The only thing that led us to think it was Satanic was the one symbol that we found on the seat of the chair. There were three, small, burnt-in intersecting lines, it's hard to tell exactly what it is. I can't find any books about this. Where are we going to get them around here? I tried the three biggest bookstores in Casper, and they don't carry that kind of stuff.

The symbol is one line straight up and down and then a line crossed over so it looks like an *X*. It could be an inverted cross; it could be something else. Who knows? But we can't figure out why this was built in the middle of nowhere. It's built out of lumber that looks like railroad ties except they're not soaked in creosote [wood preservative].

Some of our guys said the table could be an altar. Well, I'm not going to say that for sure.

There's a pit dug in the middle of it.

When I first looked at all this I thought maybe somebody wanted to have a permanent picnic table, but there's no pop-tops, no trash, no nothing. If it's a picnic table, they've done a real good job of cleaning up, and people around here don't usually do that.

It's not too far from a little town that used to have a lot of people in it back in the eighties during the boom. Now it doesn't hardly have anyone. There used to be a uranium mine, but since we don't use that anymore, they closed the mines around here. There's maybe twenty or thirty people living out there, but you can't see the site from the town. It's down in the gully.

It looks fresh. Where they put this stuff up, grass hasn't grown up around it yet.

As I say, this is way out in the middle of nowhere, but we had another site, one that we know more about, which is near town, about three or four hundred yards up in a gully from one of our elementary schools. We found it because there's a housing addition nearby, and some people saw a fire out there one night.

[Undersheriff] Don Clemens and the local chief of police went out there and found five kids. I talked to one of them and he said it was no big deal. One of them had painted himself with blood, and he said it was just a kid prank. He said he was using his knife to carve a piece of wood. It slipped, and he cut himself so he decided to use the blood to paint his face. That's what he told me.

At that site they had stuff spray painted all over the rocks. Most of the stuff is plain old graffiti like you and I used to write when we were kids plus names of metal groups like Satan's Host, Motorhead, Metallica. They had the names of songs. There were also Satanic symbols like the pentagram, "666," a lot of upside-down crosses. They were spray painted black.

They had built a pit out of river rocks. In the fire pit we found some animal bones. We found some nooses made of baling wire. They were about a foot long; you couldn't hang anything with them. They called the area Devil's Island. Right above it they have a sign that says Satan's Coven with an arrow pointing to the fire.

We have had animal mutilations. We had two horses that were stabbed. They weren't killed. All this started during the fair. One of the horses was cut up pretty bad. Those kids were in the area during the time; they could have done it, but we have reason to believe—because of whose horse it was—it could have been some other motive, some other person.

About two weeks earlier, we had a horse hurt in a corral area. It was in a ten-acre area called the Glenn Addition where it's just corral after corral. The guy didn't report it because he didn't see that much to it until he heard about these other horses being hurt.

We've had some cats and rabbits being killed in this same area; their heads were cut off.

I have reason to believe that some older kids may be involved, maybe nineteen- or twenty-year-olds. I don't think any adults are involved.

We're still looking into it, keeping our eyes open.

DET. PAT METOYER: There is a lack of reporting of incidences. There are probably the same number of incidences, but in the past, as you walked by the wall that had a pentagram, you would jump on the phone and call the police, "There's a goddamn Satanist living in my neighborhood." With the news media and the flood of information we received with the Night Stalker, the heavy metal groups, and people who want to put labels on records, people began to associate that pentagram or upside-down cross with album covers. Now they begin to look at it as something other than a threat. It's just a kid painting something on a wall.

For example, there was a school in the Valley that was closed because of decreased enrollment. There was a white flight as parents sent their kids to private schools. The abandoned schools became perfect playgrounds for kids. In addition to playing, kids went there to do rituals.

I had a meeting with a fellow from the unified school district who had three schools that had been entered. Once entered, one of the skeletons that had been used for classes was taken into the auditorium and a huge pentagram had been drawn. The bones were laid out in a formation. He wanted to know if it meant anything. He hadn't taken pictures, and he hadn't secured the area so by the time he came back the cleaning crew—which cleans about once a week or so—had cleaned up all this crap.

It's in a quiet neighborhood and you would think that somebody would call if they saw candles burning in the closed school, but maybe people are thinking, eh, it's not a big deal. With all the coverage in the news media it has a tendency to minimize the severity of what may have occurred.

The Cemeteries

Cemetery thefts and desecrations are considered one of the most heinous crimes by society. Often, youngsters who want to express their anger in the most destructive and provocative way will vandalize cemeteries and mausoleums. Sometimes the destruction is done for a different reason, however, by adults as well as teenagers.

DET. PAT METOYER: We had a case of a guy who broke into the Hollywood Mausoleum, where Rudolph Valentino is buried, and after causing $6,500 worth of damage crawls two hundred feet down this dark, damp corridor to take a head out.

Why wouldn't Hollywood Memorial cemetery press charges of felony vandalism for desecrating these tombs? Why? Do you want somebody to know that your loved one is placed in a cemetery that they can't control? That's the bottom line. That's why so many cemetery desecrations go unreported or misreported.

In East Los Angeles, in Calvary Cemetery, every Saturday the 14th the grounds keeper has to right tombstones. Some son of a bitch has been trying to dig up bodies. The grounds keeper excuses it by saying it has to be Friday the 13th dares. Why does it have to be Friday the 13th dares? Why can't it be someone who is there to steal bones, which is in fact what happens.

People stole the left hand of a man who was buried. It's called "the hand of glory." In the old days they would take the left hand, dry it and then light the fingers on an altar. This pays homage to the devil, because the left hand is the path of the devil and the right hand is the path of righteousness. This gave the devil absolute domain. It's his light. This is exactly what these people were doing. Why else would they take the left hand? The guy also took the ashes of a female who had died. We asked him, "Why did you take the ashes?" He said, "I didn't really want the ashes, I wanted the box." We know chivalry isn't dead. His wife doesn't have a jewelry box, so he was getting her one. He said he was going to dump the ashes out, polish it up and give it to his wife. Come on.

We booked him for health and safety violations, desecrating a cemetery. In interviewing him later he said he was a Satanist. What did he want the head for? He said, "For my rituals."

San Francisco Chronicle, Feb. 11, 1984

FIVE DEVIL CULTISTS ARRESTED IN THEFTS OF HUMAN ASHES

Newport Beach

Five suspected devil worshipers have been accused of burglarizing tombs and stealing human remains, possibly for use in Satanic rituals, police said yesterday.

Detective Gary Traina said the case was "the weirdest thing" he has seen in 11 years of police work.

The first of the thefts occurred December 22 at Pacific View Memorial Park in Newport Beach when two urns, containing the remains of a man and his wife were taken from a mausoleum.

The second theft occurred January 29 in Redlands, about 60 miles northeast of Newport Beach, where vandals stole a pair of urns, also containing a couple's remains from a mausoleum at Hillside Memorial Park.

[Gary Traina is a detective with the Newport Beach, California, Police Department.]

DET. GARY TRAINA: The incident started with two break-ins and robberies of cemeteries in which burial urns were stolen. Redlands police called us and said they had a couple of similar cases and wanted to come down and talk with us. We had some suspects but nothing firm.

One of Redlands' patrol officers had stopped a car with some kids in it, and he noticed that on the front seat was *The Satanic Bible*. He mentioned that to the detectives, and they contacted me because the kid was from around here. I knew the kid. After questioning him for several hours, he copped out to stealing the urns with two other kids here and in Redlands.

He told us that he was the high priest of a coven. He was seventeen and proud of the fact that he was a high priest at such a young age. There were about seven people in the coven.

He said he and his group used the remains for their high masses. We recovered one of the urns, but didn't get any of the remains back. If you're familiar with cremation, the ashes are actually bone marrow that's been ground down into a fine meal. That's actually what's in the urns. It's not skin or anything like that. Then they put an ID tag on it. We were never able to identify whose remains they were.

They performed their rituals on an island that was in the upper back bay of Newport Beach. It's a man-made dredging place where the back flow from the ocean comes into the bay. There's a lot of bamboo and high growth, about six to twelve feet high. These kids had gone out there and nicknamed the island Neco Island which they said means death in Latin or Greek. We even found drawings and maps of the island in his girlfriend's parents' house.

We found traces of some kind of sacrifice there. We found

blood, but we weren't able to discern if it was human blood, because it had been burned. We found clothing.

I don't know if they really got into the human sacrifice. They admitted to having sacrificed small animals. With rains and high tides any remains would have been washed away anyway.

The water was about six feet at the deepest point. They used a bunch of Styrofoam and made pontoons for rafts. At high tide they would float out there. During low tide they would use the rafts or wade out. They went mostly late at night.

They said they were doing the high mass. They also said they were engaged in sexual acts because much of the mass, as you know, is lust-oriented.

They had dug a pit about four or five feet deep and covered it with bamboo. Just by walking by you would not have seen it.

There were upside-down crosses made out of bamboo that they had tied at the entrance to warn people away. The actual altar was like a barbecue grill that they had made out of some wire. On the sides of it you could see burned candle wax, black and red.

It was interesting to me because nothing like this had hit here before. I was the one with the case, and so I tried to learn as much as I could about the subject. San Diego County and Riverside County have had a lot of active cases involving both white and black Witchcraft. A lot of the information that we get is from the white witches.

All the kids were placed on probation. We had to be very careful what was said because of lawsuits. If you were just basing the case on their religious beliefs, you had better watch out.

DEPUTY PROBATION OFFICER DARLYNE PETTINICCHIO: I talk to kids who tell me, "I need a human skull for my ritual." The skull is supposed to be magickal; it holds a lot of power. One kid told me that he would kill somebody to get it or he would just steal it from a graveyard. Cemeteries are vandalized and broken into all the time by kids. Some do it just to raise hell, but some do it because they need body remains. I hear these things all the time.

I've seen kids who carry body parts, like fingers, around with them for the power they're supposed to contain. Yeah, it's nuts, but the kids believe in it.

CAPT. DALE GRIFFIS: Cemeteries are prime targets for Satanists. Many of them believe that the power remains in the skull. They need body remains for their ceremonies. I get so many calls about cemeteries that it has become commonplace. The latest thing now is aboveground mausoleums. I worked a case where they were broken into and parts taken. There was a big red *W* painted on it. I'm not sure of what that means. It could mean Walhalla.

Police departments write it off as kids having a good time, or they did it because they got drunk. Bullshit. These people know what they're doing. They've got a specific goal in mind. They need something having to do with cemeteries for their rituals. Besides the bodies, you have to remember that cemeteries are consecrated ground. Because of that, Satanists want dirt or anything else related to it so they can use it, defile it, in their rituals. Cemetery dirt is a big item. You can sprinkle it around when you're doing your ritual.

DET. SANDI GALLANT: Satanists believe that they can use the power contained in a body part. The head may contain the spirit, the heart may contain the soul. These are things that would allow them to be in control.

CHAPTER TEN:

THE LUCAS COUNTY INCIDENT

Because of the secretive nature of Satanic activity, law enforcement agencies often get only one chance to crack a case. If they miss, they may lose that opportunity forever.

The Daily Sentinel-Tribune
Bowling Green, Ohio; Saturday, June 22, 1985

HUMAN SACRIFICE REPORT LOOKS LIKE A BIG FAIRY TALE

Toledo (UPI)—A report that sparked extensive excavation for human sacrifices committed by Satanic worshippers may have been "a fairy tale," say authorities.

No sign of any human sacrifices was unearthed during two days of excavations that ended Friday at the Spencer Township location, 15 miles west of Toledo.

Authorities did, however, find several objects they said were related to cults and their ceremonies. "We'll regroup," Lt. Kirk Surprise of the Lucas County Sheriff's office said Friday. "We'll go back and try to gather more intelligence."

Both Surprise and department spokesman Marvin Reams said they doubted they would find any of the 50 to 60 bodies that Sheriff James Telb said may be buried there.

"I would assume this thing will all turn out to be a big fairy tale," Surprise said.

Officials found evidence of occult activity including a headless doll nailed to a board, a triangular arrangement of wood stakes and the remains of a bonfire.

CAPT. DALE GRIFFIS: The incident in Lucas County was a fiasco from the beginning. It was lousy police work. To understand the whole story you have to know the background, the events leading up to it, stuff that wasn't in the newspapers or on TV.

A policeman I had at one of my lectures called me about a dog that some people thought might have been sacrificed at a cemetery in Columbus, Ohio. He said to me that he didn't think the animal's death was occult-related. He said it didn't fit the parameters of what I had taught him; the throat wasn't slit and the blood was still in the body. It just happened to die in a cemetery right up against a monument. It looked suspicious, but appeared to be a coincidence. I told him I agreed.

Then he said to me; "I want you to come with me."

"Where?"

"We're going to go into the hills."

I brought my friend Mike Gardner with me because I have trouble driving long distances. We met this witch. You talk about white skin. She had the whitest skin of anyone I've ever seen. She told me about being taken as a child into the Toledo area. She said that she watched a baby sacrificed outside of Toledo in a woodsy area, just north of Bowling Green.

I have a lot of contacts in the occult world. I treat them with the respect that I give anyone else. I listen, I'm polite.

A couple of weeks later, a federal agency, who likes to remain nameless, called me and said they have a woman in an East Coast mental hospital who is talking about being in Toledo in the past year and seeing a baby sacrificed.

They asked me what I thought. I said I didn't know what to think.

Now I hear from a student of mine in Lake Township who gets information by the grapevine that there was activity in the area around Toledo and that a child had been sacrificed.

Then I had a psychiatrist call me from Southern California, who had been reliable in the past, who has a woman undergoing therapy. She had been involved with a woman who placed her child in a coffin after it had been sacrificed. She talked about activity in the Toledo area.

I've been keeping all this information in my head. There's nothing to do with it but file it away. A bit later, I received a phone call from a friend of mine who is a deputy sheriff in Lucas County just outside of Toledo. He said, "We got a problem. We've been working this case and push is to shove, right now."

I said, "What do you mean?"

He repeated himself, "Push is to shove."

I said, "Fine. It's Saturday, Marv. What the hell do you want?"

He said, "I want you in Toledo in an hour."

"You know Annie [Griffis's wife]. She's gonna kick my ass if I go up there."

"I'll kick your fanny if you don't show up."

I owe my life to Marv Reams. When I was in high school, I was operated on for knee surgery. I was given the wrong medicine when I came off the operating table. Marvin was a big orderly, and I was a big kid. His job was to beat the hell out of me so I wouldn't fall asleep. It was high medicine. He has a heart as big as anything so when he called me, I went.

The department had an informant who was inside an occult group. She said she was present when sacrifices had taken place.

LUCAS COUNTY SHERIFF'S DEPARTMENT
1622 SPIELBUSH AVE.
TOLEDO, OHIO 43624

Interview [partial]: April 22, 1985, 1745 hours

Investigation:
[Investigator will be denoted by letter I]

I. Now we would like to you to speak up as best you
can. The reason why we are here, on last Wednesday
I believe it was, the 17th of April, Mrs. Jones (pseudonym, friend of Sandy) [not Sandi Gallant] contacted me regarding some activity that has been
going on in Lucas County, Western Lucas County, for
a number of years in which there is a group of peo-
ple. I'll refer to them as a cult that worships Satan.
Right?
S. Right.
I. And part of their activities involve regular masses,
meetings, wedding rituals and, on particular days of
the year which are important to this group of people,
there are human sacrifices. Right?
S. Yes.
I. How long have you been a member of this group?
S. I came to know them in 1969.
I. 1969. Here in Lucas County?
S. Yes.
I. Okay. Did you have any prior contact with these
types of people prior to 1969?
S. Yes. The man that I married in 1965, his father be-
longed to Satan.
I. Where was that?
S. [Southwest state]

I. Was your husband a member of the group?

S. No.

I. Did he know of your involvement?

S. Yes. He drove me to the meetings, but he chose not to participate.

I. Who got you involved in the Laredo group if it wasn't your husband?

S. My father-in-law. I met a woman named Linda, and she was involved in it. I met other people in Perryville who were invited and that's how I got involved in this area.

* * *

I. How big was the group in Toledo?

S. About 100 to 200, but we broke up into groups of around 30 for our meetings.

I. Where did you meet?

S. There was a house right beside a [place of business, gave street address]. The two buildings connected.

I. This is where the meetings took place?

S. Yes. We played games, blood draining games.

I. Blood draining. What do you mean?

S. They need blood for a lot of things. When you bring somebody in for an initiation, you have to take this blood and wash them down with it. They stand on a star inside a circle, and they wash them down with this blood.

I. Where did this blood come from?

S. It was drained mostly from goats.

* * *

I. If you brought in a new recruit, how would you check up on him?

S. There are policemen, members of the cult. Their contribution to the cult would be police checks.

I. Do you have human sacrifices?

S. Yes, mostly babies.

I. Where are the sacrifices held?

S. Houses in the woods.

I. How do you prevent someone from seeing the ceremony?

S. We have guards. They would be watching for "breakers." There are three rings of guards. The first would stop somebody, tell him he's on private property. The second would try to run you off. He might take a shot at you, but it would be just to scare you. The third would kill you.

CAPT. DALE GRIFFIS: I knew things about the Toledo area from my sources that the Sheriff's Department didn't know. I had been hearing all these things in the past month or so.

I said to Marv, "That's great. I'll give you an hour-and-a-half lecture on the occult, and I'll get the hell home." So I gave the Lucas County sheriff's detectives a lecture, and I was ready to go home when Marv says to me, "We've been holding one thing back. There's going to be a sacrifice tonight. In about an hour."

We went to an area of houses near woods and open fields. I told them that if anything is going to happen it will be between midnight and 1 A.M. They had deployed the men around the perimeter.

"I'm going to tell you one last thing. The interviews talked about guards. Instead of a horn of plenty or a sword, he's going to have a shotgun. I don't want you guys going in there unless you've got a Startron [a device that lets you see in the dark] or something like that." They didn't have any of that stuff. They didn't realize they were dealing with dedicated people.

They had seven men plus Marv and me. Three people on one side, two north to us, two south of us. In the middle were woods, houses and an open area. We had agreed to meet at one o'clock.

At five minutes to midnight, the lights in the houses started going on, one by one. At one minute to midnight a dog howled and gurgled. That was all I saw or heard.

About one o'clock we made the pickup, and I debriefed these people. The guys nearest the houses were terrified. They had gone flaky. They said that at the stroke of midnight a girl screamed and they heard people—there must have been thirty to forty people—chanting "More, more, more." They were about three hundred feet away; we were about fifteen hundred feet away.

Back at the station I told them that there was something out there. I said, "Know who the players are before you move in, because if you don't, if you muddy up the waters, they'll go underground, and you'll never find anything. You've possibly got conspiracy for murder, and God knows what else."

They said they heard about another place a mile and a half away where people have been spotted in the woods, down an abandoned lane. They heard they may have been burying some of their stuff there.

The next holiday that came up, I gave them my Startrons. There were people chanting in robes and hoods, the whole bit. Sure enough, in a tree they spotted someone who looked like he had an automatic weapon. I felt better about telling them not to go into the woods on the first occasion. They would have been outgunned.

I had given a lecture in Toledo a short time later, and they came to me and said they were going in. I said, "Are you sure you know who the players are?" and they said yes. I said, "Make damn sure you do."

I'm at work, and I get a phone call from the press. They

ask, "What is your part in the thing that's going on in Toledo?" I said, "What thing that's going on in Toledo?" He said, "They're digging for bodies."

"They're what? I don't know anything about it."

I got a call from one of the cops who tells me, "We're not finding anything." I said, "What do you want me to do? You're the ones who said it would be there." I said, "Do you know what you're looking for?" He said, "We think. . . ." I started screaming at him, "What do you mean you think?"

They described the area as blocked off with red thread, black thread, and white thread. All together it was a big area and inside that area was a smaller area encircled with just black thread. It's about five hundred by five hundred and right in the middle of a thicket.

I got a call from Marvin, "Can you come up here?" I said, "When I'm done working here I can."

They sent Life Flight [the medical evacuation helicopter] for me. We get up there, make a pass over the area, and I saw mini-cam after mini-cam. I wanted to get the hell home. They had been digging for many hours before I arrived. They had bulldozers, backhoes, all kinds of equipment.

The spot where they were digging was totally new to me. It was the spot where they had seen the large group of hooded people, not far from the Michigan border. Keep in mind that Sheriff Telb did not know they were going to search that day. Marvin Reams was out of town.

The following day they tell me it's worse today than yesterday, and I tell them, "Hey, I didn't tell you to dig. Give me some space." I'm getting static from my own mayor who thinks I'm a nut and would like a piece of me.

I had my son Dale go up with me. I kick myself in the ass because I took him there, too. Ever since that day, he developed heart troubles that he got from ticks in the woods. Dale is there twenty minutes, and he finds a forty-by-twenty building they hadn't even found. The building is six foot up and in the middle of a bunch of trees. The trees have chains attached to them. It looked like they were used to chain people. There were all kinds of occult symbols on the building.

I yelled at these people, "Didn't you do a good search? What the hell's wrong with you?"

I told Telb, "Do yourself a favor. Call the search off. Get these people out of here, and I'll come back and we'll do a search. Take your lumps and let it die." Telb was set up to look stupid, I believe, by someone who wanted his job.

I got my ass kicked from one end to the other when nothing was found. I looked like a real ass, especially in the *Columbus Dispatch* a few days later.

Columbus Evening Dispatch, June 23, 1985

SATANIC MURDERS: A GREAT STORY THAT JUST WASN'T THERE

By James Breiner
Dispatch Assistant Metro Editor

TOLEDO—Hanging from a tree branch next to a rural Lucas County road was what for all the world appeared to be a piece of red string, perhaps six inches long.

It wasn't knotted or arranged in any way. It just hung there about eye level, waiting for the wind to carry it to the ground or for an expert on Satanism to call it a tool of devil worship and possible evidence of ritual murders.

Some 50 people gathered around the string last week and listened as Dale Griffis, a Tiffin, Ohio, police investigator who has a reputation as an expert on Satanism, told them that red string is used to mark boundaries of Satanic ceremonies.

Then Griffis, whose public relations polish shows his experience in dealing with the news media, did something police investigators rarely do. He led this pack of journalists back into the woods to what is known in the trade as a crime scene and displayed some key pieces of evidence gathered.

This makes great tape for television and great pictures for newspapers.

The tramp through the woods resembled a nature hike, with Griffis pointing out the sights. Investigators rarely do this sort of thing for fear of disturbing evidence.

Griffis has played a big role in investigating what Lucas County Sheriff James Telb described as the possibility of 50 to 75 ritual murders, many of them supposedly involving newborn infants in a wooded area west of Toledo.

Telb sought Griffis' advice during the three-month investigation marked by reports from several informants who said they were members of a 200 person cult. Telb had Griffis flown in by helicopter Thursday to view suspected sites.

Telb still has no bodies and no other physical evidence that any murders took place, but the reports from informants, none of who actually witnessed any killings. He stopped digging Friday but said he is still investigating.

What Telb does have is a collection of objects, some odd and some commonplace, that Griffis says are evidence of Satanic rituals.

Take the knife for example. It was found in the trash littered ramshackle vacant house a few hundred yards from the alleged mass grave sites.

The 6-inch blade has a somewhat unusual shape, slightly curved and tapering at the point. The handle is wooden. To someone unfamiliar with Satanic cults it looks like an odd kind of kitchen knife. Griffis said it is an athame, a ritual dagger.

When asked what made this knife an athame, Griffis said, "Any kind of knife can be an athame, even a steak knife."

Griffis said he has studied Satanic cults for about eight years and did his doctoral thesis on the subject. Police departments all over the country have sought his advice when confronted with examples of mutilated animals and desecrated graves as well as related drug or sex activities, he said.

At one point, Griffis led the journalists to a small plot of ground set off by several stakes with red string attached.

To the uninitiated, it might have been a failed vegetable garden, but Griffis said it was a ceremonial ground used by the Satanists. A small metal can stood in the center. Griffis said it was used for burning, but there was nothing in it.

In a vacant cinder block house near the staked area, investigators found a sheet of tin with several lines of letters written backwards. Sheriff's deputies said these are Satanic symbols, but they can't decipher them.

Also found in this area was a headless doll with its feet nailed to a board and a five pointed metal star tied to its wrists with red string. The star, Griffis said, is a Satanic symbol. A rag and a toy telephone receiver also were attached to it. Griffis said the doll is used in a death ritual.

As for the rag and telephone, he said, "I'm still trying to work that out."

For the skeptical who say that Satanic ritual murders are more rumor than substance, Griffis points to a highly publicized case in Riverhead, New York in which a teenager was stabbed to death by another teen in what was billed as a Satanic ritual.

[On July 4, 1984, police found the body of Gary Lauwers, seventeen, in a shallow grave in a wooded area of Northport on New York's Long Island. According to a statement to police, Ricky Kasso, seventeen, admitted killing Lauwers by stabbing him in the face and cutting out his eyes. Kasso said he screamed at Lauwers, "Say you love Satan," before the boy was killed in a Satanic ritual.

Kasso and at least twenty other people had belonged for several years to a Satanic cult called "Knights of the Black Circle," which had previously held rituals in which they sacrificed animals. In 1981, police found the burned carcass of a baby goat on a picnic table in a park where the group often congregated. The group also had painted pentagrams, inverted crosses, and other Satanic symbols in the park. Kasso had an inverted cross tattooed on his arm and had been arrested the previous April for digging up graves for use in rituals. He had stolen a skull and left hand from a corpse.

Also arrested with Kasso was James Troiano, eighteen, who police say held the victim down while he was being murdered. Kasso told police that Lauwers had stolen ten bags of angel dust from him.

Kasso committed suicide by hanging himself in his cell several hours after his arraignment. Troiano was acquitted of second degree murder charges less than a year later in a highly publicized trial in Riverhead. A third youth, Albert Quinones, witnessed the murder and had been granted immunity for his testimony.]

The other example Griffis used was the Charles Manson gang which committed a series of murders in 1969 in Southern California.

So far, there is no physical evidence that anything of this type has happened in Toledo.

Although Telb called off the search, he defended his action in executing a search warrant for a suspected cultist and the unsuccessful search for bodies.

He said there was information that a ritual murder would take place this weekend to coincide with the summer solstice.

"It was too early, based on the information we had, but we couldn't wait until Monday and find that someone had been sacrificed," he said.

CAPT. DALE GRIFFIS: Saturday I went back there with Marvin. We pulled up some floorboards on another house and found hatchets, knives. All had a substance on them that was red in color.

Three weeks later I put out the word to my sources that I'm angry. I want some answers. I wanted to know what was going on up there. I got back reports that we were in the right church wrong pew. I also got reports that some occult members were near the search team. Were they moving stuff out the back while we were looking at the front?

FEATHER: I've talked to enough people in the Toledo area who say there have been murders. There are bodies. They just haven't found them. They may never find them.

CAPT. DALE GRIFFIS: It wasn't made public because we wanted the whole mess to be over. After the digging incident we just wanted to let the whole thing drop.

We found seventy-two left shoes. There was only one man's shoe, the rest were women's and babies'. There was no possibility that the shoes were from a shoe store. There were no tags on the shoes. Some had signs of being a little worn from use. We found six or seven athames.

Egyptologists will tell you that they find clothes, neatly pressed and folded, in mummy cases. Why? For use in the afterlife. Egyptians believed in the afterlife. So do Satanists. In the Satanic religion, there's an important difference between the right and left side of the body. When you die, the left side of the body is for Satan; the right side is for God.

I can't tell you for sure that people were sacrificed. I can only tell you what we found.

[The Sheriff's department continues to keep the case open.]

CHAPTER ELEVEN:

THE GAMBLE MURDER

Monroe County Evening News,
Feb. 3, 1986

CARLETON, MICH.—Lloyd Harold Gamble, 17, was shot and killed in his home at 10600 Otter Creek Rd. about 11:30 A.M. Sunday. Monroe County Sheriff's deputies took a 15-year-old boy into custody at the scene of the shooting.

Sheriff's department chief investigator Lt. Michael Davison said the youth had called the department to report the shooting and was still on the phone with dispatcher Carolyn Pitcher when the detectives arrived at the house.

Friends of Mr. Gamble, a senior at Airport High School, may call after noon Tuesday in the Baker Funeral Home, Carleton, where services will be at 2 P.M. Wednesday. The Rev. Ed Mason of the Carleton Community Baptist Church will officiate and burial will be in Carleton cemetery.

Lt. Davison said the department is seeking a warrant charging the youth with murder. He is lodged at the Monroe County Youth Home where there was to be a court hearing this afternoon.

An autopsy performed Sunday indicates that Mr. Gamble suffered two gunshot wounds to the head. He was pronounced dead at the scene by Monroe County Medical Examiner Dr. David Lieberman.

Mr. Davison said detectives Bill Myers and Dick Wells took the youth into custody without incident, and he credited Ms. Pitcher for possibly preventing more deaths.

"I credit her and the rest of the people in central dispatch for preventing any further incidents," he said. But, Lt. Davison said, Ms.

Pitcher was able to keep the youth talking until detectives arrived. ''Then she told him to come out and give himself up,'' he said.

Born Nov. 5, 1968 in Monroe, Mr. Gamble was the son of George and Opal (Faulkner) Gamble.

Surviving are his parents of Carleton; two brothers, Michael of Monroe and Phillip of Carleton; two sisters, Deborah Gamble of North-ville and Mrs. Kenneth (Gloria) Hill of Carleton and a grandmother, Mrs. Dorothy Gamble.

He was preceded in death by a brother, Douglas, and his grand-parents.

[Mike Davison is the chief investigator for the Monroe County Michigan Sheriff's Special Investigation Unit. Be-cause of the unique nature of this case, Davison chose it as the subject of one of his reports required for graduation from the FBI police academy in September 1987.]

LT. MIKE DAVISON: We received a call from the Carleton Police Department, a small department in our county. They said they had been called by a young male who had shot his brother. He said his parents were due home any time and that if the police didn't stop him he would shoot them when they got home.

When the police got there, he gave himself up. He didn't give any trouble. He said his brother was downstairs in the bedroom, and when the officers went downstairs they found his body. He was deceased. He had been shot point blank, twice in the head.

Three days after the incident, the investigators had been called by the family and asked to return to the house. The parents said there were some items they wanted them to see. When the investigators got to the house, the parents brought out a green vinyl bag that had been hidden in a closet. It contained a hood, long black robe, silver chalice, dark blue candle, glass bottle containing red liquid, piece of white parchment paper, eleven cassette tapes of Motley Crue, Black Sabbath and other heavy metal groups. There were more items found under a rug. There was a book titled "The Power of Satan," a paper pentagram, a bingo card, [the card had the numbers 666 in a row] a sword, money orders, and an upside-down cross.

The book, "The Power of Satan," came from a Satanic group in Canada. We believe he got information about the group while he was at a Motley Crue concert. The book gave step-by-step instructions on how to perform a Satanic ritual. [The book is a nine-page pamphlet reproduced by a copy machine. It bore no copyright holder or author's name, but was sent by a group known as CASH, Continental Association of Satan's Hope, in Montreal.]

THE POWER OF SATAN [Excerpt]

Dear Member:

Welcome to the good times ahead!

First off, Satan and his organization would like to thank you for showing faith and solidarity. We are sure that through our mutual help of one and other we will defeat the diseased minds of the priests of the churches and temples of the world that seek to slander our mighty lord Lucifer. Eventually, our mighty leader Satan will regain his position of prominence: Those who help in our crusade will be rewarded handsomely, your every dream will be fulfilled. Those who work against our master will be punished!

In all our years of research of the different ways to make contact with the mighty Satan, our experience has taught us that the most effective way is as follows: First you must get yourself a table which will serve as an altar. Next, you need a sword to lay

on the altar. Use a long knife if no sword is available.
Next you need a chalice or goblet filled with wine.
Next you need a parchment or piece of brown paper
if commercial parchment is unavailable. Do not kill
an animal if none is available. Next you need a black
candle. As far as clothing is concerned, it is definitely
preferable to wear a black robe. If black is unavailable simply get any color, and dye it black.

Now you must wait until the sun sets and it is
dark. Next you must be totally and completely alone
in your house or apartment. Place all the elements
on the altar. Turn off the light, light the candle and
repeat:

"Emperor Lucifer master of the rebellious spirits,
I beg you to be favourable to me when now I call for
your minister the great Lucifuge Rofocale, as I desire
to sign a contract with him. I beg also that Prince
Beelzebub may protect my enterprise. O Astaroth,
great count, be favourable likewise and make it possible for the great Lucifuge to appear to me in human
form and force, without bad odour, and that he grant
me by the agreement which I am ready to sign with
him all the riches I need. O great Lucifuge I pray that
you leave your dwelling wherever it may be to come
here and speak to me."

Take a small pinch of the sacred powder and
sprinkle it over the candle and chant the following
three times:

"In the name of Satan the ruler of the earth, the
king of the world, I command the forces of darkness
to bestow their infernal power upon me. Open wide
the gates of Hell and come forth from the abyss to
greet me as your brother and friend.

Grant me the indulgences of which I speak.

I have taken thy name as part of myself. I live as the beasts of the fields, rejoicing in the fleshly life.

By all the gods of the pit, I command that these things of which I speak shall come to pass."

After you have done this, you should take the sword, hold it with both hands straight in front of yourself and state:

"Hail Satan,

"Hail Satan,

"Hail Satan.

"I call upon the messengers of doom to slash with grim delight this victim I have chosen. Silent is that voiceless bird that feeds upon the brain pulp of him who hath tormented me and the agony of this shall sustain itself in shrieks of pain, only to serve as signals of warning to those who would resent my being."

LT. MIKE DAVISON: We didn't know anything about the occult, but it was getting clearer every day that there was something more to this case than met the eye.

I knew Dale Griffis from another case. I had worked undercover in Toledo on some drug cases. It's common to use out-of-town detectives in undercover operations. I knew that Dale had been looking into this area.

We spoke on the phone, then Dale came up and looked at the evidence we had. He told us that he thought the killer was acting out some kind of Satanic ritual at the time of the shooting and that he was acting alone.

CAPT. DALE GRIFFIS: Davison did his homework. He actually read *The Satanic Bible* and found references that apparently jived with his case. I think this kid crossed over from the dabbler stage to the self-styled Satanist stage. If I was going to put him in a slot, that's where I would put him. Here's a kid who's a loner, not doing great in school, into drugs and so on. Kids who are having problems sometimes think, if I just had these magickal powers, I could solve them. Satanism is about power.

This wasn't a spur-of-the-moment murder. It was cold and calculated. I believe he thought he felt he was doing his brother a favor by killing him. He was elevating him to a higher consciousness. He had mentioned those exact words to the police dispatcher.

Mike asked me who else I would advise he talk to, and I suggested Sandi.

DET. SANDI GALLANT: I explained to Mike about the occult paraphernalia and all the other evidence. From what he showed me, the kid was into the occult. It was pretty clear that was the case and could have been the motive for homicide.

LT. MIKE DAVISON: While we were out seeing Sandi, we talked with Pat Metoyer in Los Angeles. He said, "Yes this is Satanic, but don't go to trial using that. Just say you've got a homicide. Don't say it was occult in nature." He told us not to dirty up the case. You've got a homicide. Period.

DET. PAT METOYER: I've worked homicide before, and you always go for the jugular. I said to Mike, "If you've got the gun, you got the guy who called you on the telephone, you got the whole body, why do you give a shit if he did it while he was dressed in a black robe? Who cares about the motive? You only need that if you're trying to figure out why it occurred. I know that it occurred. I've got the kid copping out to doing it. Do I really need to get into the motive?"

In a case like this, why get into the Satanism? Why plant the seed of doubt in a juror's mind that this guy is mentally deficient?

[Larry Clock is a juvenile officer with the Monroe County Sheriff.]

DET. LARRY CLOCK: Prior to this incident, we had started to get some undertones of things going on. There was the case of a boy who lived with his very elderly grandmother. He went around the house and took down all of her religious pictures. He took her crucifix and turned it upside down, and then beat the hell out of her. Sure, I can't say that he did it because of Satanism, but at the same time school officials were finding all kinds of Satanic symbols in his locker. He was making a big deal about letting everyone know that he was involved with Satanism.

About two days prior to the Gamble homicide, I told Mike we really have the makings of a problem in one of the school districts. We had a kid stomp another kid, kick the hell out of him, and then jump on the table in the cafeteria—in front of all the other kids—and start flashing the devil sign [made by holding the two middle fingers with the thumb so the two fingers point up like horns].

At some of the schools, kids were hanging up their artwork of goat's heads and baphomets along with the other students' drawings. The teachers didn't know what it meant. We were getting all this scattered stuff, but you figure it's just kids doing kid things.

One of the officers who works in the public schools as a liaison officer was actually the one who had brought all this to my attention. He brought me a stack of books from the school library about the occult. We were just beginning to study them, to see what the kids were reading, and the next day this kid kills his brother.

The next morning, we're all in the office starting to investigate this when we get a call that the arrested kid is involved in a cult. I started going through the books and come upon February 2, the holiday of Candlemas, the day that the killing occurred. It just hits you in the face. Then the parents brought in all the paraphernalia, and you have to say, maybe there's something to this.

Then, we checked the names of the kids who checked these books out of the library, and they were the same kids whose names we had been hearing in connection with the alleged cult.

LT. MIKE DAVISON: I can't go into all his statements, because he is a juvenile under Michigan law and his statements are confidential, but when he was in the youth center he made comments that confirmed our belief that he was into Satanism. It verified what we were saying.

DET. LARRY CLOCK: He made comments to his friends at school about what he was into. He made no secret of it.

[Richard Rhine was a classmate of the Gamble youth. He asked that he be given an alias.]

RICHARD RHINE: In school, he would always be telling us about Satan, and how it had helped him and how it gave him power. Some of the other kids got involved but not like Phil. He was really into it. He didn't care who knew about it.

He was obsessed with the power that he said Satanism gave him. It worked, too. The girls would be calling him all the time. They were curious about exactly what he was doing.

LT. MIKE DAVISON: We had gone through *The Satanic Bible* and matched up things that were in common with the murder and with the things he told us. Look at page 88 about sacrifices and the next page about sibling rivalry.

EXCERPT FROM *THE SATANIC BIBLE*, page 88

"The only time a Satanist would perform a human sacrifice would be if he were to serve a two-fold purpose; that being to release the magickian's wrath in the throwing of a curse and more important, to dispose of a totally obnoxious and deserving person."

[page 90]

"The ideal sacrifice may be emotionally insecure but nonetheless can, in the machinations of his insecurity, cause severe damage to your tranquillity or sound reputation. Mental illness, nervous breakdown, maladjustment, anxiety neuroses, sibling rivalry, etc, etc, ad infinitum have too long been convenient excuses for vicious and irresponsible actions."

LT. MIKE DAVISON: There are references on other pages to the timing of the homicide. They say the best time is in the early morning hours when the victim is in the dream sleep. He killed his brother in the early morning. The method is mentioned too, on page 125, "They must be shot, stabbed, sickened, smashed, burned, drowned, or rent in the most vividly convincing manner!" A shotgun blast to the head is very convincing, I'd say. What we had there in the homicide was basically right out of the book.

I'm not saying that anyone will just read *The Satanic Bible* and kill someone, but remember, you have to look at this from the mind of a fifteen-year-old. He doesn't understand what's real and what's imagery. Kids take things literally. [*The Satanic Bible* talks about killing people by proxy only.]

Shortly after the killing, we got an anonymous call about a house in the country. If you went out there, it would lead you to believe that some kind of occult activity was taking place. It was abandoned and had writings on the wall, paintings on the walls, fire pits. There were black crosses on the surrounding trees that was to keep the bad in and the good from coming in. They had done all the classic things. I can't say that rituals took place there, but all the evidence would lead you to believe that some kind of activity had taken place. We had received information that our suspect had been out to this house. He had been part of a cult, but at the time of the homicide we believe he was acting alone.

Then we had the Christians fighting the cults. The abandoned house had been set on fire. I can't say who did it, but I'm pretty sure it was the Christians. Somebody had gone out to the house and written Christian sayings over the Satanic graffiti, things like "Jesus Lives" and "Jesus is God." The next thing we knew, the house was burned down. One Christian group had a public record burning. They were burning Beatles records, if you can believe that.

All hell was breaking loose. Rampant rumors of cult murders were flying around. We wanted to stop those rumors and put out the word of exactly what happened. We wanted to let people know that this murder was not the work of an occult group but of one person. Our concern was that this would snowball. Someone else might get wrapped up in the occult, think it was cool to off someone like this, and we'd have a copycat. We hoped that by putting out a news release and holding a press conference we would put an end to some of the rumors.

NEWS RELEASE

On February 2, 1986 investigators from the Monroe County Sheriff Department began an investigation into the shooting death of an Ash township resident in Monroe County. During the course of that investigation information was received that the shooting was connected to the act of Satanic worship. Investigators began looking into the possibility that Satanic worship could exist within Monroe County.

After an in-depth investigation and after receiving numerous tips and information from experts in the field of Satanic worship, investigators feel that the shooting death was the acting out of a Satanic sacrifice. Officers feel that the subject involved in the shooting was acting on his own and not as part of a cult or group at the time of the shooting. Also during the investigation, officers have learned that students in three school districts in the county of Monroe practice the worshiping of Satan. At this time, it is not known how many are taking active part in the practice, however, it is believed to be a small number.

Due to the seriousness of the crime that has taken place, officers feel that there are certain things that parents should look for if they feel that their children are involved, that being an inverted pentagram which is an upside down five pointed star, drawings with goat heads, upside down crosses or the numbers 666 in a row. The youths might also have a black hooded robe, daggers, swords, chalices, black or white candles, and parchment paper. These are items that the youths might have hidden in their bedrooms or other hiding places. Also, heavy metal rock groups have been known to use Satanic symbolism in their acts, videos, and their music.

Lt. Michael Davison
Monroe County Sheriff's Dept.

DET. LARRY CLOCK: After the press conference, we got sixteen calls from parents saying things like, Thanks, we appreciate what you're telling us. . . . Our kid has been dabbling in it. . . . I've got this kind of stuff around the house. . . . Our kid wanted some money to buy a black robe, saying it's not for Satan but for something else. The parents were saying, Now I know what it's for. Now I can deal with my kid.

We got no negative phone calls from parents. We did get some negative calls from people saying, You're only stirring things up. We don't need this here. They never identified themselves, but I got the impression that it may be from people who were into Satanism themselves.

LT. MIKE DAVISON: We had all this evidence that the motive could only be Satanism, but we knew the judge wouldn't allow it. If he did, it would make him look bad. He had already made the comment that there was no such thing as Satanism and Devil worship. He said the suspect may have dabbled a little bit, but there's more than dabbling here. We have a killing.

Evening News
Feb. 20, 1986

"I think a lot more serious problem is [student involvement with] drugs and drinking," Judge Seitz said. [Seitz's office refused an interview with the author.]

LT. MIKE DAVISON: We couldn't come up with any other motive for the killing except Devil worship.

There was a lot of political riff between the sheriff's department and the judge. The sheriff's wife worked for the court system, and the judge she worked for retired. This judge didn't like her because he didn't like the judge that she had worked for. There had been fighting between these two judges for years. It was a terrible, terrible relationship. This judge fired the sheriff's wife, and that's when the political problems started. I believe that the judge let his personal feelings interfere with the professional judgement reference us in that case. We know for a fact that the kid believed in Satan, but the judge wouldn't allow it.

In the end, we followed Pat Metoyer's advice. We didn't mention anything about Satanism or Devil worship at the hearings.

[Because he is a juvenile, his case remains in probate court where the judge has pronounced him mentally unfit to stand trial and therefore not guilty. The boy is to remain in a mental health facility until his eighteenth birthday.]

As it turns out, some good came out of all of this. We've been getting the word from our juvenile officers that some kids who had been doing these sorts of things have stopped. This incident scared a lot of kids into thinking, This is serious stuff.

Even our road officers have become more aware. They will call in if they see something in the woods like a "666" or a pentagram. They never did that before. Other police departments call and tell us about something they've found at an abandoned house or a club house.

We had one report of a dead lamb found near a house that had "666" written on the walls. We don't know if a farmer dropped it there by coincidence or what, but it was written up as a suspicious incident report and put into a file. Maybe it will mean something later, but that's the kind of thing we're doing now that we didn't do before.

If this incident changed me in any way it changed me to feel that there are a lot of things going on out there that we have absolutely no idea about. That's a scary thought for a police officer. Just when you think you may know it all, you don't. When something that open is out there—I mean the school had those pictures on the wall—and we didn't know what it was, that's frightening. We had kids wearing upside-down crosses and nobody really knew what it meant. To have that kind of activity going on in our county and us not know about it, that scares me.

CHAPTER TWELVE:

THE OCCULT SURVIVORS

In the past few years, many children have been telling stories of being sexually abused by groups of adults in a ritualized and bizarre manner. They tell stories about seeing pentagrams, people in robes, chanting, human and animal sacrifices, praying to Satan, and other trappings of the occult. Many of the allegations came from children who were enrolled in day-care centers or nursery schools in Southern California and later other places around the country.

Because of the nature of these allegations, many people don't believe the children's stories. That's not surprising. Children make poor witnesses in the eyes of courts. Because these stories, though bizarre, are so similar to others around the country, however, officials are beginning to believe them.

Part 1 of this chapter is about the children and the stories they tell.
Part 2 is about adults who were abused as children.

Part 1

DET. RAY PARKER: Child abuse is difficult enough to deal with. One-on-one child abuse, Daddy does child or neighbor does child—that's hard. Juries don't like to face it. Nobody likes to face it.

If you go in front of a jury and say that two or more adults at the same time are doing a little child we're so into their conscious [of the jurors] to where they're totally blown out of their seats. How can anybody think of doing something like that to anyone, let alone a child?

Now we go to more than one child being molested and more than one adult doing it, and we haven't even got into the hoo-hah shit yet. All we're talking about so far is organized child abuse.

Then you get into the hoo-hah shit involving Witchcraft, Satanism, or some bizarre occult religions that most people know nothing about on top of the organized child abuse and wow . . . it just blows the jurors out of their chairs.

You get John Doe citizen on the jury who doesn't have a background in law enforcement, and it's hard for him to believe that these things are going on.

[Lawrence Pazder is a pioneer in the field of ritualized abuse and was introduced to the topic through a patient, Michelle Smith, who was then twenty-seven years old. Smith's mother gave her to a Satanic cult for their rituals when she was five years old. She was sexually, emotionally, and physically abused. Pazder, a fellow of the Royal College of Physicians, currently practices in Victoria, British Columbia. He has been a psychiatrist for twenty-one years.]

LAWRENCE PAZDER, M.D.: I coined the phrase "ritualized abuse" in 1980 at an American Psychiatric Association annual meeting in New Orleans. It was a way of trying to understand it and separate it from sexual abuse. If you try to treat them the same way you run into a lot of problems and can do damage to the children you are treating.

What I was hearing didn't fit anything I knew. It wasn't

treated in any of the literature I knew. The definition I presented for ritualized abuse was this: "Repeated physical, emotional, mental, and spiritual assaults combined with a systematic use of symbols, ceremonies, and machinations designed and orchestrated to attain malevolent effects." That definition has held up pretty well.

DET. SANDI GALLANT: Ritual abuse to me would be a systematic series of abuses that take place, usually involving multiple suspects and multiple victims. In that abuse, some type of bizarre behavior will occur that is not consistent with what we call traditional abuse. In a traditional abuse case you will find one victim and one abuser and unless they know each other it will usually occur on only one occasion. That abuse will merely consist of the touching or entering private parts of the body.

Ritual abuse cases may involve external types of tools, often a mutilation of an animal sometimes used as a way of threatening or intimidating the children. They may be taken to a cemetery, and forced to lie in a grave.

However, just because you come across a child taken to a cemetery doesn't automatically mean it's Satanic ritual abuse. Satanic ritual abuse is specific. The child will tell about calling upon Satan, perhaps chanting in a nondiscernible language, wearing robes of a specific color, use of colored candles. Candles in themselves are not always an indication of Satanic activity. That's why I always hesitate to tell investigators what to look for, because they may go out and ask a leading question.

You'll hear about the drinking of blood and sexual activity at the culmination of some ritual. That activity involves the leader of the group alone or the first one of the group in orgy fashion. Mock marriage ceremonies to me would take on a Satanic connotation in that some documentation I've seen indicates they will bring in young females and go through the ceremony as if the child is now Satan's own. You'll see the use of Christian artifacts in a blasphemous form.

I think this kind of activity has always been there. You hear it from people who are in their fifties and sixties. It wasn't categorized then. It wasn't discussed, and until five or six years ago you couldn't find victims who would talk about it. Cops didn't hold seminars on sexual abuse until recently. They held seminars on child abuse but not sexual abuse. Go to a library and try to find a book about child sexual abuse. You may find them now, but prior to five years ago, good luck. Now that we are addressing the problem, we find that it doesn't fit the pattern of what we call traditional abuse.

DET. PAT METOYER: Kids are taught that if you lose your tooth you put it under your pillow, and the tooth fairy will come and leave money. Santa Claus is a good spirit. There are many things that we tell children which pretty much is ingrained as good.

Then we tell them, If you don't be good, the bogey man will get you. Kids are susceptible to believe there is a bogey man. So when someone tells them that an evil entity will get them, they pretty much believe it. That makes it easier for ritual abusers to control kids by these bizarre methods.

DET. SANDI GALLANT: We had a case that was handled by a nearby police department. The mother had called our juvenile division because a little boy had turned up missing here in San Francisco and her daughter, Rhonda [a pseudonym], saw him on the TV and said, "My daddy and I picked up a little boy named Kevin the other day and he looks like him." There was already a sexual abuse case going on against the father.

The mother told the investigator that she would like him to talk to her daughter because she's telling some really strange stories about devil worship and stuff. He called me and said, "Would you like to go over with me?" I said yes.

The mother told us that she was divorced from her husband for five years. Rhonda was three at the time. Her husband was given visitation rights. She said that she noticed that when Rhonda returned home from the visits she was spacey and wouldn't look at her or talk to her. She withdrew into herself and stared into space. Her schoolwork was suffering, and that's when the mother thought Rhonda had emotional problems and should see a therapist.

Because Rhonda would not openly talk with the therapist at first, she began drawing pictures instead. The pictures showed knives, swords, swastikas, pentagrams, people in robes, cries for help, and a child being thrown in a fire. Some of these incidents date to when Rhonda was three years old.

The mother was totally misbelieving of what she had heard from her eight-year-old daughter about devil worship. She was a very religious woman.

When I saw Rhonda, I thought she looked like a Cabbage Patch doll, a small pudgy eight-year-old kid. She was very introverted and soft-spoken. You could barely hear her sometimes. She would talk in a whisper.

Rhonda was uncomfortable talking to us. We had her mother call the therapist, who Rhonda had a rapport with, and had the therapist come over. Other than to get Rhonda relaxed enough to talk with us, we didn't let her do any questioning. Rhonda would kind of stand there right between Rich [Det. Hesselroth] and me. She would look at us when she would answer, but she was very nonresponsive most of the time. The mother wasn't in the room during the questioning.

We started talking to her about what she had seen, and she told a variety of stories.

San Francisco Police Department
Intra-department memorandum

To: Captain Daniel Murphy
Commanding Officer
Intelligence Division
Monday June 18, 1984

CONFIDENTIAL
Satanic Cult Activity Info.
Re. Possible Homicides

From: Sandi Gallant, policewoman

[Excerpt]

Rhonda describes rituals in great detail and recalls one Halloween when they all dressed up in costumes and went to the [stepmother's house] where members of the group were dressed up in their blue robes. There were candles lit, and they all stood in a circle and called upon Satan. There were swastikas on the wall, and they would say Hail, Hail to the swastika. She recalls a picture of a dark haired man with a moustache on the wall. She says this particular night no one was hurt, but she described other rituals in which animals are killed and dismembered. She says these animals were dogs, sheep and goats. (These are the types that are sacrificed in Satanic rituals.) Knives were used in most rituals, and sometimes the children were threatened with them.

Rhonda told me that she remembers another occasion when her father picked up some children in San Francisco, and she says she believes that her father sexually molested them, and then let them go a day later. These children were not part of any group ritual.

DET. SANDI GALLANT: The story that stands out most in my mind was the one where she talks about being in a room and seeing a picture of a man with a moustache on the wall and seeing a swastika on the wall. She didn't call it that; she drew it for us. The people are in robes, and there are policemen present. She said they had blue uniforms, and she was sure they were policemen. Her father was in the National Guard, and we thought maybe they were green uniforms. She insisted they were blue. There were a couple of other kids present.

On this occasion, a man came into the room and brought with him a baby. The baby is given an injection. There is a fire going in the fireplace. They put the baby's legs in the fire. We just let her tell the story, but I did stop her every once in a while to ask questions. At that point, I said, "Did the baby make any noise?" She said, "The baby screamed."

She said they brought the baby over and put her on a blanket in front of Rhonda and Rhonda's father brought her a knife—she called it a knife and drew it for us. It looked like a dagger in her drawing. She drew the whole scenario for us in fact. Her father gave her the knife and told her to put it in the baby's belly. She wouldn't do it. Her father got behind her and put his hand over hers and put it into the belly. I asked her, "What happened next?" She said, "I saw worms come out."

My first thought was that this kid was nuts. My second thought was: how is a kid going to know that the intestines —she described them as worms—are going to come out unless she actually has seen it or has seen something that looked like it?

She talked about how they cut up the baby and drank blood. She talked about how they put the baby in a container of "smelly water." Those were her words, "smelly water."

When Rich and I got back in the car all we could say was this kid is crazy. We just couldn't believe it. There's something wrong with this kid. At the same time, we realized it was something that we had to pursue.

There was evidence of sexual abuse. Rhonda had vaginal

problems since she was two months old, but doctors had always said it was from the soap or poor sanitary habits. When she got older, a doctor at Children's Hospital determined that Rhonda had been sexually molested.

We ended up going back for several more visits. Sometimes we would just go over and buy her an ice cream to build up a relationship. Sometimes we would just drive around looking for locations. She had no problem directing us to other apartments where her dad had lived, which I thought was pretty good because some of them were miles away from where we were.

We were able to build up a relationship, and her stories remained consistent.

We tried to go out to areas around Mount Diablo where she said things had happened, but we could never find the places. I would talk about how pretty the mountain was and say, "Don't you love the mountain?" She would say, "No, I don't like the mountain." She didn't like Mount Diablo.

The police department wanted to pursue it only as a sexual abuse case without putting any of the ritual abuse stuff into it. That's always a danger, because if the defense finds out you know this stuff, or if a kid gets on the stand and starts babbling about it, you have a major problem on your hands because you withheld information.

It finally went to trial, the charge was incest, and the jury ended up hanging it six-six. Afterward, some of the people on the jury said they had no problem with the sexual abuse, but they had a real difficult time with the Satanic ritual allegations.

We had a whole series of cases similar to this case that had come over a few years' time. The kids were telling similar stories. Most were out of our jurisdiction, but I knew about them because I was being asked to consult by other agencies. I told the boss that we wouldn't get involved in any cases unless asked to do so by the outside agencies. I told him I thought I was beginning to see a pattern among the cases.

I sat down with the boss and said I would like to write a synopsis on each of these cases and send it to the FBI. I said, "If there is something to it, then that would be the appropriate place for this information to go." We had tried to get the DOJ [Department of Justice] to look at it, but if it's got anything to do with religion they don't want anything to do with it. At least to your face, they tell you they don't want to know anything about it.

I did the synopsis and submitted it to my boss with a note that I would like him to review it and send it on to the chief. That's the chain of command. I said that because of the nature of the material I would like it forwarded to the FBI.

The chief came back to me six months later with a copy of the report in his hand. Now remember, this man and I had been friends for twenty something years, and he says, "Do you really want me to send this to the FBI?" I was pissed. I was really upset.

When the chief gave me back that report, he looked at me and said, "Do you really believe this stuff goes on?" Like I said, this man and I go back a long way, and we've always had an extremely close professional relationship. One thing he's always given me credit for is my tenacity and that I'm not one to spin wheels for nothing. If I think there's something there, I'll stick with it.

I got to tell you, this really disappointed me. I know how difficult this stuff is to believe. I know it because I've been where he was at that point. I remember listening to Rhonda and saying to myself, give me a break. Yet, at the same time, I've seen other crimes that have been committed that are every bit as heinous. . . . Gacy . . . how much more gruesome can you get than burying little boys underneath your house? [John Wayne Gacy was convicted in 1980 of murdering thirty-three boys in the Chicago area from 1972 to 1978 and burying them in and around his house.]

I don't know why the chief didn't want to submit it. I don't think he was trying to save me any embarrassment. We were close enough that if he thought I was off my ass he would say, "Sandi, you're really out to lunch here, and you need to see a shrink." I don't think it was that. I think part of it was lackadaisical. Probably at first he looked at it and said, "Shit, it's twelve pages. I'll just put it over here and read it later." He probably forgot about it because there are other things that are more important—which I understand.

Memorandum
San Francisco Police Department

To: Captain Daniel J. Murphy
From: Officer Sandi Gallant
Date: February 14, 1985
Subj: Ritualistic Child Sexual Abuse

Sir,

Attached is my report on cases of Ritualistic Child Sexual Abuse which have surfaced in the past ten months in the State of California and elsewhere. I have either participated in the interviews of victims or assisted outside agencies in the analysis of the information and have determined that, very likely, the information contained herein is true.

It is requested that the report be forwarded to Chief Murphy for his review and then to SAC Robert Gast, FBI. This is merely a synopsis of case information. Copies of case files will be submitted to the FBI with this report upon approval.

Sir,

I wish to bring your attention the following information which was developed during an investigation by this division. Although the information
contained herein pertains to organizations apparently involved in Satanic worship, it should be noted
that the investigations are not concerned with the
beliefs or legal practices of those groups. These investigations only pertain to alleged criminal activities
conducted by individuals who happen to be affiliated
with certain groups.

INTRODUCTION

During investigations of cult activity, conducted
by this division over the past several years, information was coming forth that numerous adults involved
in the traditional practice of Satan worship were
veering off into an area of criminal activity involving
the mutilation of animals, drinking of their blood,
and partaking of specific organs of their bodies for
ritualistic purposes. In the summer of 1981, further
information from sources close to practicing Satanists revealed that some of the Satanic groups were
getting involved in the murders of children and
adults as a part of their religious practices. Until recently, none of this information was able to be confirmed by law enforcement officers. In May 1984, I
had occasion to interview one Rhonda Smith [pseu-
donym], WFJ [White Female Juvenile] 8 years, regarding activities she was forced to partake in with
her father. These interviews revealed information
possibly linking her father to an apparent organized
crime group of people who are involved in the drug-
ging and sexual abuse of children and their possible

witness to and involvement in multiple homicides of other children and adults.

The information contained herein is distasteful and bizarre, to such a degree that one would choose to discredit it. However, research that I have done in this area has revealed that numerous cases of this type are surfacing around the country and in Canada. The similarities in the stories of each child victim used in these crimes tend to give credibility to the information revealed by others. Additionally, the psychiatrists and therapists who have been treating the victims state that the consistency of the stories and the explicit details revealed cause them to believe that these children are telling the truth. It is also the belief of each law enforcement officer who submitted information for this report that the victims are being truthful and that, in fact, children would be unable to make such stories up.

During my research, similarities began surfacing which indicate the strong probability that there exists a network of people in this country involved in the sexual abuse and possible homicides of young children. These cases appear to differ from isolated cases of abuse towards children in that the crimes mentioned here have been committed with one common goal in mind—that of mutilating and murdering children for ritualistic or sacrificial purposes. Many of the cases reported also reveal the possibility of child pornography beyond the normal type of "kiddie porn" in that these children are photographed during rituals with some members in robes or other garb and candles, snakes, swords, altars and other types of ritualistic material being used.

In order to substantiate the credibility of this information, I am including the following case histories from contributing police agencies throughout the country that are currently in the process of either investigating or attempting to prosecute such cases.

It should be kept in mind that these are merely synopses of the cases, and not all detailed information is being submitted at the present time.

It is requested that this report be reviewed by Chief Murphy. At that time it should be submitted to Agent John Minderman, FBI Office San Francisco, who will forward it to the National Center for Analysis of Violent Crime at Quantico, Virginia. I have been in contact with Ken Lanning of the FBI Behavioral Science Unit who has agreed that these cases fall within the privy of the NCAVC for review and analysis purposes.

Respectfully submitted,
Sandi Gallant Policewoman #1918

ATHERTON, CALIFORNIA CASE

DATE OF OCCURRENCE: 1984-1985
VICTIMS: 1 WFJ
AGES: 17 years
CHARACTERISTICS:
Forced into S&M sexual activity with stepfather and friends. Photographed in sexual situations. Observed animal mutilations. Drugged occasionally by injection. Drank blood. Observed homicide of WMA 30 yrs. Subject suffocated, knifed and then suspects removed heart, legs and possibly his penis. Dead cat found in victim's school locker after reporting incident to police.

DOCUMENTATION: Police reports, Child Protective
Service Reports, interview.

ACCUSED/CONVICTED:
1 accused—stepfather
10 other suspects
No charge brought as yet.

FREMONT, CALIFORNIA CASE
DATE: 1985
VICTIM: WMJ
AGE: 5 years
CHARACTERISTICS:
Subject states he is picked up at school by an adult
and taken to a house and possibly a church. He is in-
jected with something that makes him drowsy.
Forced into sexual activity with at least two men,
sometimes being photographed during same. Black
candles observed in room. Observed the mutilation of
animals and human beings.

DOCUMENTATION: Police reports

ACCUSED/CONVICTED: 2 suspects, none accused as
yet

FT. BRAGG, CALIFORNIA CASE
DATE: 1985
VICTIMS: 7 Juveniles
AGES: 5-7 years

CHARACTERISTICS: This incident occurred at a Day-Care center run by [a local] church.* Pentagrams and black candles were observed by the children. Forced to drink blood and urine. Knives were used to kill dogs and cats. Children would be locked in closets. Saw things and possibly animals suspended from ceiling. Children were injected with something and photographed during sex. Victims observed the homicide of one infant.

DOCUMENTATION: Police Reports

ACCUSED/CONVICTED: None accused as yet. Suspects are sisters and one worked at preschool. Daughter of one suspect may have lured victims.

REDWOOD CITY/LIVERMORE, CALIFORNIA CASE
DATE: Unknown
VICTIMS: WMJ, WFJ
AGES: 13, 8 years
CHARACTERISTICS:
Black candles were used during rituals. Satanic chanting heard and black robes worn by adults. Children were injected with drugs and photographed during sexual activity with adults. Claimed to have observed the murder of a small child (2-3 years of age). Victim was hit on head, stabbed and arms and fingers removed prior to child being thrown in fire. Male victim claims room "really stunk."

DOCUMENTATION: Police reports

*The name has been withheld as the case is still open.

ACCUSED/CONVICTED: None accused. Agency refuses
to follow up.

KING COUNTY, TEXAS CASE
DATE: Unknown
VICTIMS: 8 juveniles, 2 WMJs, 6 WFJs
AGES: 4-15 years
CHARACTERISTICS:
Victims were sexually molested and allegedly photo-
graphed during sexual activity. They observed skele-
tons, cauldrons, ropes and knives during rituals.
Were forced to devour body parts. All were injected
with drugs and forced to observe homicides of at
least one adult and one child. Claim victims were
buried.

DOCUMENTATION: Police reports, medical reports

ACCUSED/CONVICTED: 10 adults accused, 7 identified,
3 unidentified. None charged, as yet.

SACRAMENTO, CALIFORNIA CASE
DATE: 1982
VICTIMS: 3 WFJs, 1 WMJ, poss. 5 others
AGES: 3-9 years
CHARACTERISTICS:
Mother was drugged and children were drugged then
taken from their home where the mother was allegedly left sleeping. Children were sexually abused by
suspects, taken to graveyards and laid in open
graves. Forced to take part in animal sacrifices and
the homicides of three children. Photographed during
sexual activity. Homicides may have been photo-

graphed as well. Victims observed black wall hangings in room where rituals took place.

DOCUMENTATION: Police reports, medical reports, psych. reports, interviews

ACCUSED/CONVICTED: 5 suspects, including victims' father, arrested and awaiting preliminary hearing.

DET. SANDI GALLANT: As an investigator you sense the frustration, and you really start to scrutinize yourself. Am I nuts? Am I imagining these things? Am I wasting my time? What's really helped is the networking, talking to people like Cleo [Wilson] and Bill [Wickersham]. In the early days it was those two, Larry Roberts in Omaha, and a couple of other investigators in Canada, Ken Sprouse, Wayne Douglas, and Joe Brochez in Victoria. That was my network . . . and my partner Jerry. It was tough when Jerry retired, because even though I was the more aggressive worker, Jerry kept me balanced. I really appreciated that in him. Jerry is not a bullshitter when it comes to work. If he didn't see anything, back in 1979 in that original case, he would have said, "This is bullshit."

DR. LAWRENCE PAZDER: If we're talking about the orthodox Satanic groups, a cop once expressed it best to me: These people hate God. God loves little children, and they use the children to get back at God. That's one of the issues. It's central to their belief system. They want to take that soul, twist and turn it against everything that is good. The goodness of a child is attempted to be turned around. That's one issue.

The other is that it's a power trip for these people to try to turn a child around. It's carrying out the battle with God. Children are written about, especially in scripture, as being much closer to God.

The next part is that it's part of an indoctrinating process so they will be so turned against the value systems that they will be part of that group in later life. It's a very high investment in the future. Some people I have worked with talk about being tracked. They get phone messages to indicate that someone is still tracking them. It's not like there are thousands of children that they're doing this to. It's not like that. It's an investment of two to three years in each child, and they do keep track of them.

Many of these children are recontacted around age twelve to fourteen, and they are brought into the cult on a more formal basis at around age twenty-eight or so.

DET. P. J. LAWTON: What I've noticed is a complete perversion of normal moral values, trying to turn the kid completely around from what we consider moral. I wouldn't say that the cases I've looked at have all been Satanic, but I question where does the Satanic break off and maliciousness take over. They all seem to have similar things in common. I have to believe that all this behavior is part of a national pattern somehow.

[Sgt. Rod Carpenter is with the Contra Costa Sheriff's Department. He began to handle occult cases as an outgrowth of his work with juvenile gangs.]

SGT. ROD CARPENTER: There's two ways to look at this. First, ritual abuse and pedophilia can be part of bona fide occult activity [sex magick, for example]. The other is that these people, who are involved in pedophilia, are just using Satanic activity to cover up. You can scare the socks off a five-year-old just by playing weird music or wearing a black robe. I can't tell you which it is. My guess is that it's probably somebody playing the part of a Satanist, doing the ritualism, but you never know.

DET. PAT METOYER: If you attempt to prosecute a person for a sexual abuse, and if you want to bring in the fact that there is ritualism involved, you run the risk of losing your case. I am on call for the L.A. County District Attorney's office as the resident expert on ritualistic abuse. When they have a problem they call me. I will tell them what it is I think they have.

I invariably warn them also that unless they want to open up a can of worms I say, Why do you want to bring up all this other material? why do you want to bring up how this child was abused? However, that's for individual cases. For large scale abuse cases, you may want to show a jury some scheme and design in the abuse.

Some of what goes on at rituals is illusion, just to scare the kids, but I do believe babies have been sacrificed.

LAWRENCE PAZDER, M.D.: A child can have fantasies, and can have imagination and should have those things if they've been through a horrendous situation. It's not that they're fantasizing about that experience—they can do that too—but while they are in the experience they have to escape through fantasy. When they are relating that incident to you they may talk about a puppy playing with a ball or having an imaginary friend. They don't necessarily separate the real incident from the fantasy.

When we take these children before the court, and they start talking about their fantasy world that makes the judge think, well this kid is making it up. But they have to retreat to the fantasy world to deal with the reality. If you can hear that and help the child know that you are able to understand that then they tell you with fairly good discernment what was fantasy and what was real.

DET. JACK FRASIER: We have one case of two brothers, ages seven and four, who are in a hospital. The grandfather is high priest of the coven. Grandmother runs a nursery school in another state. The mother is in there, too. It's a generational thing.

We were called in because the nurses in the children's psychiatric ward were hysterical because of what the kids were saying, doing, and drawing. One kid was drawing a picture of his nurse all cut up and in a pot cooking. He was sitting there telling her that he wants to cook her and eat her. This is a seven-year-old talking. The four-year-old describes how to get rid of bodies. The kid doesn't even know how to read or write and he's describing three different ways to get rid of bodies.

First, the group will eat the body parts, two, they have dogs that eat parts of the bodies and third, the kid says a crematory.

He describes perfectly how a crematory operates. I had never been in one so I went to one to check it out. He not only described perfectly how to do it, but when they do what, precisely, step by step.

He also described another way to get rid of bodies which is quite ingenious. They go out to a cemetery the day before a funeral and find a grave that has been dug. They dig about a foot down more, put the bodies they want to get rid of in there and just cover it up lightly. The next morning, the cemetery people come out there for the burial—nobody looks down there—and buries the body. Who's ever going to find out? I've heard this a number of times, but this came out of a four-year-old. That wasn't something he read. He doesn't know how to read. He participated in it is what I'm saying.

The programming of these kids is intense. When the grandfather sends them a get well card it has a seashell taped to it. When the boys see that, they try to kill themselves. Every time they were abused there was a seashell around. When they see that, it's a signal to kill themselves. Another patient tries to kill herself when she receives a red carnation. It's all programming, and it's different for each person and each group.

LAWRENCE PAZDER, M.D.: One of the problems with this, it's that it gets your own imagination going in an attempt to figure these things out. I find that a dangerous thing to do. I try to listen to only what I'm told by those undergoing the experience. If that experience coincides carefully with what someone else has told me I give it a little more credibility. You really have to be careful with this stuff. There isn't a Satanist around every corner. Quite frankly, I think it's a way for people to deal with their own fear about the area and try to handle it and project it out there at the same time.

Like our own book [Pazder and his patient, Michelle Smith, co-authored a book, *Michelle Remembers*, about her experiences and healing], you have to be careful that people aren't using that to trigger their own fears and feed on the material in there. It does encourage a degree of paranoia, because you can't put your hands around a lot of this stuff. I think there is a high risk of flakiness out there. You have to keep your feet solidly on the ground and keep listening to what is there and keep comparing. Drawing a lot of conclusions isn't what's important. What's important is to hear and collect the information and make sense out of it. I've been doing this for nine years, and I'm just as careful now as I was when I began. When you hear someone finding it all over the place that's their own problem, part of their own inner psychopathology.

What is important is not to give the power of fear to these things anyway. It's an area that as soon as you get caught up in the fear you lose it, because then you have to deal with that fear in some way. If you believe in Satan, if you believe in evil, then you have nothing to fear anyway because you also believe in Jesus. I challenge the people who terrorize the Christians with talk of Satan. If you go the other way, if you don't believe in Satan, then you have nothing to fear.

This is a hard one because the media, the movie industry, everyone is very eager to capitalize on this and get the fear going and make it dramatic. I've seen all kinds of movies that do that. We've turned down millions from people who want to turn our book into a movie, because we can't get control over the final cut. We would want them to make it in a balanced way, not just to touch people's terror.

Remember that we all have a place of terror inside. If these things touch that then we have to handle it. We apply it to all kinds of occult things to give meaning to things that aren't there. This is used in ceremonies with the children. They encourage this kind of fear to make it seem as though they have certain powers. That they can alter life with their powers. For instance, they'll have a piece of flesh and put electricity on it to show children that they've got power to make it jump. It gives terror to a child to make it seem like they've got this power that's bigger than they are.

DET. SANDI GALLANT: We had one mother whose daughter we believed to be ritually abused. The medical records bore it out, and so did other evidence. The problem was that the mother kept parading her around to talk shows and like that and every time she did, the child changed her story. What happened was that every time a new ritual abuse case came up, the girl started to tell the same story as the one who was just abused. The mother and daughter became highly suspect. That's a shame, because it took away from their original allegations, which were probably true.

JUDY HANSON: The problem with all of this is that everybody gets real paranoid about this and says, Oh no, they're drinking blood and eating hearts. I'm sure some of them do. It's a big world out there, and people do whatever they feel like they want to do. But until you actually see them do it, you can't say they do it.

I'm not going to go around looking for witches and warlocks and things that go bump in the night. Damn it, I'm not going to say something's true unless I know it is, but I've got children here who are describing high rituals. These are children who are describing the same things, and neither they nor their parents have had contact with each other. Most of them still don't, by the way.

I've been concentrating on the cases involving the pre-schools in the South Bay area around here. People have heard of the McMartin preschool case, but eight preschools have been closed in this area.

[The McMartin preschool case brought to the attention of the public for the first time allegations about ritual abuse on a large scale. The stories that some of the children told were bizarre, and few parents—let alone law enforcement officials—believed them at first.]

COUNTY OF LOS ANGELES
SHERIFF'S DEPARTMENT
OFFICIAL CORRESPONDENCE
February 10, 1985
FROM: BETH DICKINSON, SERGEANT
SEXUALLY EXPLOITED CHILDREN TASK FORCE
TO: AGENT KEN LANNING, FBI ACADEMY
BEHAVIORAL SCIENCES UNIT
QUANTICO, VIRGINIA

SUBJECT: LOS ANGELES COUNTY SHERIFF'S
DEPARTMENT
PRESCHOOL INVESTIGATION

In August 1983, the Manhattan Beach Police Department began an investigation regarding allegations of sexual abuse occurring at the McMartin Preschool. A 2 1/2 year old male was the first victim to disclose being sodomized by a male teacher at that location. Subsequent investigation revealed numerous additional victims. Altogether, approximately 400 children were evaluated by therapists at Children's Institute International. All interviews were video-taped and 350 children disclosed sexual behavior; 49 did not.

In all, the victims named seven teachers (six women and one male) at the preschool as having molested them. These individuals are currently charged with 209 counts of child molestation. Also named are about 30 other individuals still uncharged, as well as numerous unidentified "strangers."

McMartin victims allege sexual abuse occurred on school ground as well as at a local market, churches, a mortuary, various homes, a farm, a doctor's office, other preschools and other unknown locations. They also talk about being taken on airplane rides to unknown locations.

The forms of alleged crimes are rape, sodomy, oral copulations and insertion of foreign objects. Most children state they were photographed in the nude. They talk about various games being played that involved being naked (both children and suspects) and involved some type of fondling. Some of the games mentioned by the children are the Naked Movie Star Game, Alligator Game, Cowboys and Indians Game, Horsy Game, Doctor Game and the Tickle Game. They mention drinking a red or pink liquid that made them sleepy. They talk about the Circus Horse where the people dressed up in animal costumes. Other costumes mentioned were clowns, witches, and devil like costumes. Children disclose animal sacrificing (bunnies, ponies, turtles, etc.) and say some of this occurred in churches. Victims describe sticks put in their vaginas and rectums and also being "pooped" and "peed" on. Children say that the adults sometimes dressed in black robes, formed a circle around them and chanted.

In May 1984, another preschool investigation began in the same policing jurisdiction stemming from a McMartin victim who identified the Manhattan Ranch Preschool as a place where he was taken and molested. Then a student currently attending Manhattan Ranch disclosed being abused sexually by a 17-year-old male aide. Since then, additional children have begun disclosing sexual abuse (approximately 60) and they have named six or more additional suspects, mainly women teachers at the preschool. These victims talk of strangers coming to the school and molesting them, being taken off campus and molested, being photographed nude and some talk of animals being abused. The children talk of being hit with sticks and of being "peed" and "pooped" on.

Initially, this case was investigated by the Manhattan Beach Police Department who turned over the McMartin case to the District Attorney's office. After charges were filed on the original seven suspects it became clear that the resources of the police department and the District Attorney's office were not sufficient in order to follow up on the multitude of uncharged suspects in both preschools. Therefore, the Los Angeles County Sheriff's Department was requested to come in and take over the investigation for the purpose of investigating the uncharged suspects in both the McMartin and Manhattan Ranch cases. The Task Force became operational on November 5, 1984. It should be noted that the Task Force has two other preschools under investigation for alleged sexual abuse in addition to McMartin and Manhattan Ranch. One, the Learning Game Preschool, is

clearly linked to McMartin. The other, Children's
Path Preschool, is not. Currently the Task Force is
made up of nineteen investigators, two sergeants and
one lieutenant. In addition to the District Attorneys
who are currently prosecuting the charged suspects,
there will be two District Attorneys assigned full
time to the Task Force in the near future to provide
legal assistance and to assist in filing additional
criminal charges.

[Doctors found that the two-and-a-half-year-old male,
whose testimony began the investigation, was sexually molested. His story was tainted, however, when he said that,
along with being molested, he saw a baby decapitated and
that one of his abusers could "fly." Other children told equally
bizarre stories, many of them spoke of activities that appeared
to be Satanic in character.

After an eighteen-month preliminary hearing, charges were
dropped because of insufficient evidence against all but two
defendants, Raymond Bucky, twenty-nine, and his mother
Peggy McMartin Bucky, sixty. They were charged with one
count of conspiracy and ninety-nine counts of child molestation of fourteen students.

Three years after the first inquiry, the case went to trial
in July 1987. During the hearing, defense attorneys had tried
to prove that the prosecutor had intentionally withheld evidence of the mental instability of Judy Johnson, the mother
of the child who sparked the investigation. Johnson died in
December 1986 of a liver disease. At this writing, the trial is
still going on.]

JUDY HANSON: It's amazing to me that these children will
say things like, "I hate the sticks."

"What do you mean you hate the sticks?"

"They always put sticks in the little girls' vaginas and in my bottom. I hate the sticks."

Now you can't say this is what they did, but the children tell you that they did this with them all standing in a circle, and they all had robes on and they were all singing these funny songs that they couldn't understand the words to.

What I began doing is that I went out and bought the real easy lightweight books about the occult and the Black Arts. I've got a couple of Aleister Crowley, but who the hell can read and understand him? I have a couple of hundred books, and so I go back and look at the books, and it dawned on me that the sticks may be ritual wands. You can't perform a ritual without a wand. It has to be wood, too. I would say to the kids, "Was it a regular stick?," and they would say "No, it was more like a tree limb or a twig." That's it [a ritual wand] exactly.

I have one child, she's about nine years old, who drew a man who was sacrificed on the cross. She drew the heart in the middle, slightly to the left. She has the rib cage where it should be, and she's got two blue lungs under the rib cage. How do you know the lungs are blue unless you've seen them? [Physiologists describe the color of adult lungs ranging from blue to slate/grey. The older the person, the darker the color.] She's got the blood pouring out and the man crying, because that's what she saw.

[The following is an excerpt from testimony given to District Attorney's investigators by a five-year-old boy who claims to have been abused in a Southern California preschool when he was almost three years old. Medical reports show sexual abuse. The questions and answers have been turned into a narrative. The matter is under investigation.]

Excerpt from Testimony to District Attorney

There were five of us, two boys and three girls. They made us take off our clothes, because we were going to play a game. They called it the circle game. We all made a circle and [the two women] stood in the middle. They had black robes and sticks. They touched each of us with the sticks on our backsides. They put the sticks inside and it hurt. They also put it in the girls' fronts. While they did that, they sang a song I didn't understand. It sounded like praying from the church.

[One of the women] took a hamster from her pocket and gave it to me to hold. Then she took it back quickly and put it on the floor on a plate. She said some more strange words and cut the hamster's head with a knife. She said that if anybody told what we did, she would do what she did to the hamster to our mommies and daddies. I started to cry. So did [girl next to me]. I didn't look at the other kids.

Another time we played the circle game, they lit candles in the middle. They were black. There was a star in the circle. [The boy drew a pentagram.] They sang a song with words I didn't understand, and made one of the girls suck her titties and her front. They made all of us watch. Sometimes when we played the circle game, [the two women] told us to touch each other's private parts. I didn't like any of this.

One time they made me drink water that made me sleepy. All I remember is a man touching my private parts, and then I went to sleep.

I finally told my mommy that I didn't want to go anymore. She said, "Why, don't you like it?," and I told her about the circle game. She didn't believe me and brought me to the doctor. After that she said she was sorry and that she believed me.

JUDY HANSON: One universal story, something almost all of them talk about, is cooking the baby. This is one story that goes throughout. I make it a point not to ask them direct qustions. I try to be real sensitive with the kids. They usually begin talking about cooking the baby, boiling the baby, or cooking body parts. This is the thing that made me believe.

I didn't ask myself did they do it? I asked, Why would they do it? Did they eat it? The kids said most of the time they did not. Well then, why would they do it? I don't care if you're the craziest person in the world there has to be a reason why you would do something. Even if it's a crazy reason.

I was reading through some books one day, not looking for that necessarily, but I picked up a book by Erica Jong. She wrote *Fear of Flying*. I mention that in my lectures only because people have heard of her and that book. She's written a book called *Witches*; it's out of print.

One of the things you'll find, if you look up in the index under *flying*, is a recipe for flying ointment. Witches fly; they really do, but you have to understand their language. They fly depending upon the kind of drug they're using. As you read through the recipe for flying ointment—I've checked and found this in other books, too—one of the ingredients is belladonna. When you're done cooking this down you mix it with the oil of your choice. You can use butter or safflower oil or you can use baby fat. Now where else are you going to get baby fat?

The major question, of course, is why aren't there any bodies. There should be, right? The kids describe dead bodies. This question always comes up when I lecture to law enforcement people. My answer to them is, Oh, then you believe Jimmy Hoffa is still alive?

To get serious, however, when you're done doing whatever you're doing with the body you burn it. Three ladies in my neighborhood are into ceramics, so is my daughter-in-law's mother, and all of them have their own kilns. Nobody would notice it, and if you're out in the country nobody would notice the smell.

Several of the parents with kids in different preschools in South Bay told about the children celebrating Halloween in May. They thought that was real creative, no structure and what a neat thing. It was weird, but that was okay. The kids were supposed to have a good time.

I kept thinking that there had to be a reason for that. Why not during Easter or in the summer or something? Why May? I found a reference to the fact that the Catholic Council of Toledo [in the eighth century] took All Saints and All Souls day in May and moved it to the day after Halloween. [The original day was actually May 13.] They did that because of the Druid practice of human sacrifice during All Hallows Eve. They [the Church] did that to block the spiritual power that was brought up and pushed out into the world by the Druids. Remember, you're dealing with eighth-century minds here. That left a free day in May and what better day to bastardize than a once holy day. So we've got children practicing Halloween in May. Do you want to bet that somebody stumbled on to that and decided to use it? If they really believed in the power that would be a supreme day.

Oddly enough, the surveillance I did on these people in South Bay, the only time that none of them were home was the evening of May 13.

DET. JACK FRASIER: At seminars, one of the questions that always comes up when we're talking about nursery schools is, Where were the parents? How could these people get away with it? How could the kid go to school for a year, and you'd never know he was being abused? I would say to myself, what kind of parents are these? Don't they bathe their child, don't they talk to them? I was critical of that until I met the parents, and I met the kids. Now I believe it could happen to my kids, too. It could happen to anybody because of the intense programming and, in some cases, drugs.

The cases we really watch closely are divorces where the mother wants to get back at the father and claims that he has sexually abused the kid in some bizarre way. Now that law enforcement people are starting to understand these kinds of crimes, they perk up when they hear it. We had one case where the mother had done some research into the topic, and she was trying to say that this was all Satanic and so on. It really was just another way of getting at the husband.

FEATHER: I've heard that some kids are inducted very young. Even preschool age. They're given a doll that's laid down on a table and they're told, "Stab this. If you don't do this, this is what will happen to you."

The kids are scared. This is an adult telling them what to do. They are taught to respect an adult's opinion, to listen to adults. They are taught to respect all adults whether it's their parents or not. These poor kids don't know what to think.

These kids are told, If you don't do what we say, we'll kill your mom and dad. What else are these kids going to do?

LAWRENCE PAZDER, M.D.: It's a very difficult area for doctors because it can appear, from the stories they tell, that the child is going through a psychosis. The stories are very bizarre. Very often we don't want to hear them so we consider them a pathology. We treat the symptoms. That's one level. Another level is that most professionals, psychologists, psychiatrists, social workers, are trained not to believe in belief systems. I use the word belief system instead of religions because that's a sacred area; you don't touch it. But by doing that you avoid dealing with the belief system within that person. If you don't deal with it the child won't bring it up unless you want to hear about it. If you don't do that then you won't know what the child is dealing with inside.

If you're not understanding what the child has been led to believe about Satan or evil or believing who they are or who people are, then you can't begin to heal what happened.

Of great importance is bringing out the information, the prevalence of it, the knowledge of it. The more cases that are brought out, understood and recognized the more people will begin to make sense out of it.

Up until now, people haven't had the opening to talk about it. One of the things we hear a lot in the calls we get is, no one will even listen to us about what happened. That's changed in the last six to eight years.

There is a place in children, way inside, where they have a sense of what is right and wrong. They retreat to that place when they're under assault. It's hard to describe but children describe it as a tiny warm spot. It's a core place. It's a place of safety. Some people describe it as a soul. It's a place that we all go into when things don't feel right. It's a place way inside. Children retreat into that place as do adults, but children have a much greater access to it. With adult therapy sometimes you're working to get back to that core.

We also have to realize that children who have been there don't necessarily end up with multiple personalities, with borderline or antisocial personalities. The most interesting thing in all of this is how strong the survival is in a child. They have a deepening sense of how to survive.

You must understand what has been damaged. What has been done to their belief system. You have to allow the person to go through the experience with you in extreme detail with all the feelings, with the terror and the pain, with someone they trust so they feel connected to humanity. Many of these people are alienated. They feel those experiences were the whole world. If a child has been placed in it he feels that's the way the world is.

It's a very painful painstaking process. You have to see where they've gone and work with them at that level. Part of it is going through the pain and agony, the other part is going through the integration. You must help them know who they are, know that they can still be contacted, that they are still loved, that they are not evil and not tainted. They have to know that it's okay to hold someone's hand, that they won't tear it apart. This doesn't take weeks or months; it takes years.

We're not that clear today about little children. There are a lot of them under treatment around the country, and we don't know what will happen to them later in life. We don't have that kind of experience yet. We don't know what will happen to these children ten or fifteen years down the road.

Part 2

Only recently have adult survivors of Satanic cults come forth to tell their stories. Many have kept quiet for fear of being labeled crazy or paranoid because of the stories they tell.

[Joy Childress, fifty, has been a high school teacher for twenty-six years and lives in Tucson, Arizona. She is currently undergoing therapy. Because of the pain she feels when telling her story, this complete interview was done by letters and phone conversations. Childress does not have multiple personalities.]

JOY CHILDRESS: I have been in and out of therapy ever since my marriage fell apart twenty-two years ago. Even before I was married, I had several brief encounters with counseling. I couldn't seem to function well in my personal life. I've never had any problems functioning on a professional level, just my personal life was messed up.

Last April or May, 1986, memories started being triggered in therapy—memories about being abused ritualistically by men in black robes. Ever since then, one memory after another has come. It's been extremely painful to relive these experiences, but I am pulling through it all.

I have one brother eight years older than me. I have memories of him being involved, but he denies it. I have a sister who is fourteen years older than me. I have memories of her being involved, but she also denies it. Neither of them have ever been to therapy.

I was in the Satanic cult from birth until I was twenty-one years old. My whole family was in the cult. It was generational as my grandfather on my mother's side also participated. My experience deals with ritualistic rape, ritualistic sacrificing of children and dogs, mainly German shepherds, ritualistic eating of flesh, feces, vomit, and urine, and ritualistic drinking of animal or human blood.

In the cult I grew up in, the men usually wore black robes with black hoods, similar to the Ku Klux Klan, and it was the men who usually took charge of the ceremonies. We had a high priest who was the father of us all. It was a family cult —made up entirely of families. At one time, the high priest was an ordained Baptist minister of a prominent church in Denver, Colorado. The cult didn't have a name, as far as I know.

Some of the ceremonies were for sexual purification in which a child was raped by all the men. They would form a circle and chant phrases to Satan then gang rape the child until the child either vomited or showed so much terror that he or she would lose control over his bodily functions. Then the vomit, urine, and feces would be used for the rest of the ceremony by ingestion.

Some of the ceremonies would be performed to gain Satan's power through the terror of the child. The child would be starved, tortured, and raped in order to gain that power.

Some of the ceremonies were strictly for sacrificial killings for Satan. The child would be killed with a knife through the heart while a cult member was raping the child. The point of all this was to have the sexual climax at the point of death of the child. The terror of the child and the sexual climax seemed to give the ultimate in control and power and this power was supposed to come from Satan.

Some of the killings were put on, staged, not real. I was supposed to have killed my brother at one point, but it was really another child made up to look like my brother. Other killings, however, were real.

The bodies were always burned. Some of the bones were kept as implements for the ceremonies. I have one memory of a place where we lived in Denver where there were certain places in the backyard where I was not permitted to play. I vaguely have a memory that some bones were buried there.

Most of the meetings took place in basements with dirt floors. Some of the meetings were in barns with dirt floors. These were on farms near my grandfather's farm. There were pits in the dirt floors where they would burn the bodies. I remember that these meetings took place every Friday and Saturday night.

I was at the threshold many times believing that I was going to die. Other experiences included dismembering bodies and burning them. I was buried in a coffin with the dismembered remains of a child.

I left home with the clothes on my back when I was twenty-one. I had an aunt who helped me. She and her husband would only let me stay at their house one night because they were afraid. She found another place for me to stay, took two weeks' rent on it and said, "You're on your own."

These things do upset me very much when I talk about them, but people need to know and understand that these things really did happen and are still happening. I am working with a good therapist, two of them in fact, so I am being helped.

[Emma Williams, thirty-five, is the pseudonym of a woman who appears to have been ritualistically abused as a child. She has worked her way through the memories with the help of a pastoral counselor. The following is from the notes of the counselor released with the patient's permission. The counselor says that it is common for ritualistically-abused children to turn to God or Jesus as a means of healing, because, as children, they often have an image of someone who saves them. Often it's a religious image. They grew up in a world with mystical images and tend to find strength in similar images as adults. Williams has multiple personalities.]

EMMA WILLIAMS: My mother's father abused all his children, the boys and girls. I was born because my grandfather raped my mother.

My grandfather took care of me often. He built a loving sexual relationship with me. We had oral sex and sodomy. I didn't think anything was wrong in it.

When I was about six, I was brought to a morgue and placed on a stainless steel table. My grandfather was a mortician. There were other men there. They were dressed like priests. I had no clothes on. My hands were tied so that my vagina was out and exposed.

My grandfather lit a torch and heated up some prongs. When they were hot he placed them in my vagina. The pain was almost unbearable. He was chanting from a book.

There was a huge bowl, next to me and in the bowl was a baby. The men began chanting and bathing the baby in the water. The baby was screaming. It had black hair. They took a skinny knife and slit the infant. There was a lot of blood. They held the baby over me and the blood went all over me. The people were all covered with blood too, and they began eating the baby's guts. I was crying. I kept going in and out of consciousness.

I heard my grandfather pray: [This was brought out during a hypnosis session with a therapist.]

"Oh holy one of the world, we offer this child as a living sacrifice for your power and glory. We dedicate this virgin of God, make her holy by fornication, molestation, incest, cannibalism and torture. With this we offer her up for the purpose of High Priestess of the holy order of Satan to be used at will by all members of the priesthood especially our holy one."

The last thing I remember was my grandfather taking the baby's testicles and shoving them in my mouth. After that, I blacked out.

When I woke up, I heard people moving around me. A big silver door, like a freezer door, was opened and a big tray pulled out. The smell in the room was awful, and it burned my nose and eyes like alcohol or smoke does. The men shut the big door and turned some knobs. Then they began cleaning the room.

I blacked out again and woke up in my grandfather's house. My vagina was bleeding and my grandmother helped me stop the bleeding by using a sanitary napkin. I stayed several days until the bleeding stopped.

A week later, my grandfather approached me again. When I refused to be his lover, he put a pillow over my head and tried to suffocate me. I made believe I was dead by lying real quietly. I didn't breathe until he left the room. When my mother came home, I ran to her and began crying. My grandfather died several months later.

I don't think she knew what her father had been doing to me all those years, but over the next few years, my mother began beating me. My father wasn't aware that my mother was beating me, and I'm sure that he didn't know about grandfather and me. Father had always been very good to me and loved me very much.

At fourteen, I had an abortion and a nervous breakdown.

The abortion reminded me of that incident in the morgue with my grandfather.

I found Jesus at the hospital, and through him I am getting better. That was ten years ago.

[Ted Gunderson is a private investigator in Los Angeles. He retired after twenty-five years as a special agent with the FBI. He has investigated cases of Satanic activity and ritual abuse in connection with the well-publicized murder trial of Army doctor Jeffrey MacDonald. MacDonald argued, unsuccessfully, that a Satanic group murdered his family.]

TED GUNDERSON: A good defense attorney can make adult survivors look like fools. Their testimony is suspect. But just because someone tells you a bizarre story doesn't mean that it's not true.

DET. JACK FRASIER: The point we're at now is trying to sift through all the information and verify it. The problem we have is that a lot of the information we get is from people who are in mental institutions.

We started talking to a lot of psychiatrists and doctors and we found that the medical community was shocked when they compared notes about their patients. A doctor would say to another doctor, I got a patient telling me about cutting up babies, eating babies, doing this and that. What a weirdo, eh?

The other doctor would say, Wait a minute. I got a patient saying the same thing as yours. Then they would discuss what their patients were describing and find that they were talking about similar things even though the patients didn't know each other.

Some doctors we've been working with now believe they've been treating people for a mental illness when actually the things they're saying may be part of a program they've put into so nobody will believe what they're saying.

Some of these people have been programmed from the time they're born. Some allegedly have blood put into their baby bottles to get them used to the taste of it. Through their growing years, their parents start touching bases with the mental health community so the children have a history of having some mental difficulties. Later on, if they are sent to a mental institution it's not considered odd. Their credibility is zero.

Every adult [survivor] that I've dealt with is a multiple personality. That behavior, doctors believe, can be induced by mental cruelty and drugs.

[Timothy Maas, Ph.D. is a pastoral counselor in Huntington Beach, California. He is licensed by the state of California to operate a Marriage, Family, Child Counseling practice. He was working with Lutheran Social Services, where he was able to form long-term relationships with patients, when he first encountered victims of occult activities. He has had experience with multiple personalities stemming from childhood abuse.]

DR. TIMOTHY MAAS: About two-thirds of the women and twenty-five percent of the men who see me, for any reason, have been molested as children. They may have other issues, but molestation is often a part of that. A fair percentage of those are victims of cults, many of them Satanic cults.

I was shocked the first time, four and a half years ago, when a lady began to tell me that she would see herself in a ceremony and there were hooded figures doing things to hurt other people. I was skeptical except that she wasn't telling me these things matter-of-factly. She was sobbing and in a complete panic.

She was a multiple personality, a result of being horribly abused. It's common for people who have been abused to become multiples.

There are generally three ways to understand multiple personalities. One way to view it is as a dissociation, which technically it is. It's a dissociation caused by a traumatic event, maybe a series of events, that occur when a person is just slightly older than four or five years old. If a child is say eight years old, and a neighbor grabs them and forces them into a cult activity where they see someone killed, an animal killed, splattered with blood, forced to drink blood, buried in a tomb or something else traumatic they may take that onetime experience and bury it. Afterwards, they may suffer from headaches, nighttime fears, fears of a particular type of character, fears of blood—you get that type of reaction. It's a dissociative reaction. They don't have a distinct personality, but you may find them thrashing around at nighttime, having nightmares or huddling in a corner.

Second, if you back it up a bit, earlier in childhood, if you have a parent who takes the child and permits someone, say a relative, to take the child into the cult, maybe selling the baby into the cult, you have a different situation. The child learns very quickly that he has an area of life that is very painful. He may have times with his parents that are extremely good and times that are extremely painful.

The child of an alcoholic may have a similar kind of relationship with the parent. When the parent is sober, he's really quite friendly and nice. When they're drinking he may become violently enraged. Sometimes it's reversed.

The child learns that he must divide up the world very distinctly. It's called splitting. If the splitting is so impossible for the child to reconcile, and if it starts at an early enough age, then the separation becomes complete, and you have the origin, and later on the full development of, a multiple personality.

The child may say the only way I can relate to mother is to be mother's child. To relate to father is to be daddy's girl.

If daddy is a child molester then this particular personality will be daddy's girl who has sex with daddy. There may be another personality that is the cult child, that participates in the cult's activities, the witch child. There may be another child that's the school child, or the church child. You learn early enough in childhood to fragment yourself to take care of situations that may come up again. Usually, there are three or more personalities. Sometimes you'll see cases of eighty or ninety personalities. It all depends upon how early and complete the fragmentation is.

One of my patients had a personality named Kooah whom she used to relate only to an Indian child in school. The situation didn't come up again until ten years later when she was in college and sat next to an Indian. It's incredible, but a personality may rest inside until it's needed.

If you take it to the third category, at least as it relates to cult activity, the cultists have known about multiple personalities and its effects for probably hundreds of years. Only in the past ten years have modern psychologists clinically understood multiple personalities, although cultists have known about it much longer. They have formalized it now to where they can literally create multiple personalities. They will take children and make them multiples by forcing them to have a good world, a bad world, and all kinds of variations. They will use drugs, hypnosis, and even electric shocks to accomplish this.

There is a notorious psychiatrist in this area [Southern California] who is said to have done this sort of thing for the past thirty years. He uses the Satanic pseudonym of "Sid." Appeals have been filed all the way up to the Attorney General, but it's almost impossible to get victims to testify against him. It's very difficult to get tangible evidence to back up the claims. [The Attorney General's office of California had no comment about allegations involving someone named "Sid."]

There are burial sites with no bones. I had one patient describe three or four children being killed, put on a big heap with wood and burned. The ashes were washed down the drain. That's not an atypical story.

I think people are becoming more open to accepting these stories, because it's coming from so many places.

DET. JACK FRASIER: It takes a long time for these things to come out. Most of the people we talk to in mental institutions don't go in there for ritual abuse, they're in for other reasons. It takes months for these things to come out, and then you have to have someone qualified to recognize the problems and treat them.

I treat these people as confidential informants. In police work, you go on the theory that about eighty-five percent of what informants tell you is probably exaggeration. The rest you have to sift through and get what you're looking for in a way that you don't suggest anything to them. If you say something like, does this activity go on in Houston? they'll say, Yeah, Houston. You can't say that. You have to let them come out with it.

We've been getting a lot of information about occult holidays. We think we discovered a correlation between Easter week and occult-related crime. From Palm Sunday to Easter Sunday is the week for killing babies. We watch for kidnapings and that sort of thing. The patients we're dealing with have told us that babies are killed during those days. One person said she has seen six babies killed during that time period.

These groups don't always kidnap babies. Some have doctors within the group who will perform the birth and not fill out a birth certificate. Then when they sacrifice the baby they're not really killing anyone who existed. That's one of the explanations for the fact that we hear so much about killing babies but don't have the reports of kidnaping to back it up.

Before we say something like this, it has been verified

with a minimum of five separate people who don't know each other, who have never spoken to each other. Minimum five people. Some of these people have to be sedated during Easter. It's a bad, bad week for many of them.

JUDY HANSON: When I first ran into adult survivors about seven or eight years ago, it took a while to realize that you can be crazy and still be right.

I don't like the adult survivors as far as their credibility is concerned. They have a piece of information that is very good, but by the time they get through trying to make their point they're so desperate to be believed that they build on it and magnify it and change it around so that it's no longer credible.

I keep away from adult survivors. They don't usually make good witnesses. The funny thing is—I'm not denying what they say.

CHAPTER THIRTEEN:

THE FUTURE

Just as those who investigate occult crime have different approaches to the subject, they differ on the future of this area of law enforcement. Some see it starting to take on the tone of organized crime rings. Others see it embracing the political violence of the far right. One thing is clear: More incidents of occult crime are being reported, and police are beginning to understand it better each day.

It is still new, however, and they have a long way to go.

DET. CLEO WILSON: We've gotten to the point where police agencies around the nation have at least heard about these kinds of crimes. They may not know a lot about it, but when they come upon something that seems to be occult-related, at least they know what to look for. That's gratifying to me.

SGT. ROD CARPENTER: Occult activity has become more secretive. It's like the old street gang days. You could pick a home boy out by the red handkerchief in his back pocket. You can't do that anymore because every cop in the country would say, Hey, I know you're a gang member because you got that red handkerchief in your back pocket. So then they wear an earring or something like that. As soon as the cops get wind of that they'll switch to something else.

You go out and give a hundred talks to the PTA about

occult crime, and what do the parents do? They say to their kids, you can't wear the black fingernail polish, you can't have that *Satanic Bible*. . . . So what do the kids do? They don't wear that stuff anymore, and they hide the books. It used to be that you could go into a room and find all the heavy metal stuff and occult paraphernalia, but the parents have made the kids get rid of it. It does some good, too, on some kids. But there'll always be that one percent who you can't do anything with, who will be into occult activity no matter what you do.

DET. PAT METOYER: With increased awareness of occult crime, as we educate people, there's going to be a decrease. On the other hand, once you begin to bring this topic to a surface level, easily available to a great majority of people, then you have an increase in activity. Those persons who were not aware of it are going to become aware of it, and this will lead to an interest in occult crime. Yes, I would say that it's going to increase throughout the United States, then it will reach a peak. When it will reach that peak I don't know.

I can tell you that I've been getting many more requests to speak about the subject. Interestingly, I'm getting calls from the corn belt, from the bread basket. Occult crime has always been a problem in the east and west, but now it's spreading, moving everywhere. There is a great hunger among law enforcement agencies for this information.

The purpose of all the seminars is to educate officers about occult crime. Hopefully, this will give people ideas on what to look for so that several years from today when these crimes occur—probably with greater frequency—someone can look at what they've learned about the signs and so forth and understand what it is they have to do to handle the case.

DET. P. J. LAWTON: Most people would go to a site and possibly see something occult-related and not really recognize it. I'm trying to convince the training center to give me a couple of hours in the spring during service training to introduce the Department to some things to look for.

CAPT. DALE GRIFFIS: One of the reasons we're seeing a rise in occult activity is that the officers know what they're looking for. Before, they had looked over some of the indicators, but now they recognize them. I hope that in a couple of years the need for my type of lectures will cease, that officers will be knowledgeable, more proficient and understand what they're looking for.

I'm asked to give lectures daily. I turn down a lot. I may give a couple of one-dayers a few times a week. Or one three-dayer a week. It depends upon logistics.

The interest is increasing. I get a foot of mail a week. Telephone calls range from zero to twenty-five a day. I try to respond to each inquiry; I do what I can do.

DET. SANDI GALLANT: What we really need is for law enforcement agencies around the country to share more information among themselves. They don't do it enough.

Also, there needs to be a central depository where occult-related crime can be handled. The FBI is the logical place, but they haven't expressed an interest in doing it. They do it for other crimes, but not for this.

As far as ritual abuse is concerned, I don't think this area of law enforcement will get the attention it deserves until one of their own [a police officer's child] is involved. I think that's what it takes with these things. I don't think anything touches us until it touches us personally. It's always that it happens somewhere else to someone else. It never happens here because you don't want to admit that it goes on in your community. Certainly, you never want to admit that it's happened to me. If one of their homicide guys ends up with a kid that's been ritualistically killed they'll never stop looking for him, because it's one of their own. That may sound one-sided and distorted, but you get to the point where you think that it's going to take that much.

DET. P. J. LAWTON: Ritual abuse is such a secretive thing that I've only come across whiffs of stuff. So far our homicide people claim that there is no such thing as ritualized homicide. As long as they claim that attitude they'll never look at a homicide as being that, and I wouldn't get a chance to examine the scene. I'm working on trying to change that thought pattern.

We've got one education program planned. I recently spoke with the Coordinating Committee for Sexual and Domestic Violence. I'm slowly but surely working it in. I don't want to cause anybody to go on a witch-hunt and start looking for things that aren't there. I just want to make them aware of the potential and see if they can take it from there.

DET. BILL WICKERSHAM: There are little groups practicing here and there, but there are adult groups who practice the Black Arts networking with each other nationwide. This religion is coming back and coming back in a big way. All you have to do is go into an occult store and ask around. Look at the bulletin boards. Many groups are using electronic bulletin boards, too, to communicate on a national level.

Satanism is big money. Satanism is selling and people are buying. If it's not big business now, it will be in a couple of years. It's going to be big bucks.

DET. SANDI GALLANT: I don't have any evidence that there is a network of Satanic cults. Some people believe there is, but I haven't seen it. There's always the possibility of child pornography or drug rings that use Satanism, and those could be nationwide, but as of right now, I haven't seen any evidence of that.

DET. RAY PARKER: Right now we're looking at a case that involves a nationwide S & M cult that practices Satanism. We know that they're active on the east coast and the west coast. We believe they're using a Satanic network to facilitate the distribution of child pornography and children-for-sale activities.

DR. CARL RASCHKE: My thesis is that Satanism is often used as an ideological bonding mechanism for an increasingly sophisticated network of international criminal activity. Law enforcement isn't going to make any dent in Satanic practices by running around looking for animal sacrifices in a pasture. That's just the tip of the iceberg.

TED GUNDERSON: Satanic groups are into drug distribution in a big way. It makes sense, too. You've got the mechanism already set up, and people predisposed to doing illegal activities. I can't prove it, but this is what my informants tell me. It's not farfetched, though, is it? During the Vietnam War, drug dealers who were in the military used bodies of soldiers to smuggle drugs back from the Far East. Is this any more hard to believe?

OFFICER TIM BOYLE: We need to know more about the organized adult groups. These are the groups we know very little about.

We're beginning to see a connection between Satanism

and what we call hate-violence incidents. We would find occult symbols mixed in with swastikas and racial slurs written during vandalism incidents.

I really believe heavily in our county's Human Relations Commission. There are a lot of problems in the area as far as race relations are concerned. For instance, the Klan is still around, resurgence of the White Patriot Party and the Identity groups coming up. Montgomery County has a real good record with human relations. They're very strict about it, and I work closely with them.

We all sat down and tried to figure out the connection—why this was going on. I theorize that to write a swastika to scare a third generation Jewish person isn't that big, but when you couple Satanism with it—which is a fear that most people have—you have increased the impact of that swastika. It means something now.

Two girls in one of our schools—one was Jewish, the other was Catholic, both friends—received a threatening note about her being Jewish. Also within the note were things about Satan. Using occult symbols gives more of an impact to what they're trying to get across.

This is an area that I'm becoming increasingly concerned about. We're beginning to see hate-violence incidents wrapped up with Satanic symbols. We keep track of hate-violence incidents. We also track Satanic incidents that included hate-violence. We're seeing it. It's just coming up, and we're keeping track of it.

DET. MIKE DAVISON: We had that one major case in our county, the Gamble homicide, that was clearly Satanic. Because of that I get calls all the time to talk at seminars and give lectures. Sometimes people just call to get my opinion about a case they're working on. I always say no, mainly because I don't consider myself an expert in occult crime. I always refer them to someone with a lot more experience than me. But what that shows me is that police all over the country are having trouble with this area of law enforcement, and they want someone to tell them what's going on. The need out there is great for this kind of information.

GLOSSARY

Altar: A table used for the practice of the occult. In Satanism, it may be a nude woman.

Ancient One: The officiating priestess at a Black Mass.

Anthropomancy: An ancient form of human sacrifice.

Athame: Ceremonial knife.

Baculum: Wand, staff.

Balefire: Ritual coven fire.

Baphomet: Goat God, often used as a symbol representing Satan.

Bell: Used to begin and/or end ceremony.

Beltane: Occult festival on May Eve; also called Walpurgisnacht, night of April 30. Time for planting crops. Celts performed fertility rites and others offered human sacrifices. In Christianity, May 1 is Apostles' Day.

Bind: To cast a spell on someone or something.

Black Magick: Magick used for evil, usually to injure or kill.

Black Mass: A negation of the Catholic Mass in which black candles are used instead of white; prayers are said backwards. The communion may consist of drinking blood instead of wine and eating flesh instead of the usual host.

Blessed Be: Used by witches as a greeting and farewell.

Blood: Thought by some Satanists to contain a person's life force.

Book of Shadows: A diary of occult activity. It may chronicle a coven or an individual.

Botanica: Store that sells herbs, potions and paraphernalia for use by those who practice *Santeria*.

Candlemas: Occult festival held on February 2. Also called Ormelc. Celebration of the coming of Spring. Festival of the Blessed Virgin Mary in Catholicism.

Cephalomancy: Divination using the head or skull.

Chalice: Cup used to hold libations for ceremony.

Church of Satan: Satanic church founded in 1966 by Anton LaVey, high priest, in San Francisco.

Circle: Magick is done inside a circle for protection and/or concentration of power. May be any diameter, but nine feet is the traditional size.

Clan: Group of occult practitioners. It may contain any number of people, but thirteen is preferred. (See also Coven.)

Colors: Various colors are used in occult ceremonies depending upon ritual being observed.
   Red: Blood, sex magick, energy, life force.
   Green: Nature, restful, serenity.
   Blue: Sadness, water, tears, vigilance.
   Black: Darkness, evil, Satan.
   White: Purity, innocence, goodness.
   Yellow: Money, power, glory.

Coven: Group of occult practitioners. (See Clan.)

Covendom: Many covens believe their influence extends three miles. This sphere of influence is called the covendom.

Covenstead: Where the coven meets.

Craft: Shortened form of Witchcraft, often spoken of as "the craft."

Crowley, Aleister: One of the most influential and notorious Magickians of the British nineteenth-century spiritualist movement. He is noted for his sex-magick rituals.

Demon: Evil spirit less powerful than Satan but often helping him.

Devil: See Satan.

Familiar: A spirit who aids a witch, usually found in the form of an animal. Cats are favorite familiars for witches.

Gnostics: Religious group in first century B.C. in Europe, that had a dualistic view of the world: good versus evil, matter versus spirit. They had a god of matter and a god of spirit and elevated the evil god of matter to prominence setting the stage for the modern view of Satan as the entity with dominion over indulgence.

Goat: An animal often used in Satanic sacrifices, because it's thought that Satan sometimes takes that form. It probably stems from the Bible's story about scapegoat.

Grimoire: A book of spells and rituals telling the ways to conjure spirits. It may be personal or belong to a coven.

Halloween: Occult holiday, All Hallow's Eve, October 31, end and beginning of Celtic year. In Catholicism, November 1 is All Saints' Day.

Hand of Glory: Lighted candle placed between fingers of dead person's hand. Sometimes the hand itself is dried and the fingers are lit.

Head: A being's power is thought to be centered here and thus is a potent seat of magickal strength.

Initiate: New member of a coven.

Inverted Cross: Upside-down crucifix, often seen at occult sites.

Kabbalah: Ancient Hebrew white magick of numerology and quest for knowledge.

Lammas: August 1, festival day, beginning of harvest season.

Left Path: Generally thought to be the Devil's path, or wrong side of God. The Catholic Church in medieval times thought left-handed people did the Devil's work.

Lithomancy: Magick using stones or semi-precious gems. Colors of stones are important to working. (See Colors.)

Magick: A way of influencing nature or people by supernatural means, often spelled with a "k" to distinguish it from sleight-of-hand magic.

Magister: Male leader of coven.

Necromancy: A way of conjuring power from dead spirits sometimes using their bones, burned ash or any other part of corpse.

Occult: A body of knowledge that is hidden or secret in the area of the supernatural or paranormal.

Orishas: *Santeria* gods, syncretized with Catholic saints.

Pagan: Someone who worships the natural gods. Paganism may have been mankind's first religion. Pagan literally means a "hick" or country dweller and was mainly used in biblical times to describe someone who was neither a Jew nor Christian.

Pentacle: A pentagram within a circle.

Pentagram: Five-pointed star, which is the most important occult symbol and probably the oldest. For most occult groups it is a positive symbol depicting the four elements (fire, water, earth and air) surmounted by the spirit. The pentagram also symbolizes the perfect man, the head at top, arms to either side and feet at bottom. Satanists have turned the pentagram upside-down to negate its positive nature, seeing it as the descent of spirit into matter, also a negation the Holy Trinity because the three points now face down.

Right Path: Generally thought to be the positive side of God.

Ritual: A standard form of ceremony usually to invoke a deity.

Santeria: Worship of the Saints, a mingling of African tribal religions and Catholicism established by African slaves brought to the Americas and Caribbean.

Satan: Chief of the fallen angels who opposes God.

Shaman: Witch or medicine man in Native American and other religions.

Skyclad: Nude. Some occult rituals are conducted skyclad to enhance the summoning of power.

So Mote It Be: Words said at the end of an occult ceremony. Similar to "amen" in traditional religious services.

Talisman: Power object, usually an amulet or trinket.

Vernal Equinox: Occult holiday, March 21. Day and night are the same length.

Voodoo: Religion derivative of *Santeria* mainly found in Haiti and, to some extent, in New Orleans.

Warlock: Often described as a male witch although many of those in the craft now use the word *witch* as describing both male and female practitioners.

White Magick: Magick used for benevolent purpose, usually to heal or to help.

Witch: One who practices magick.

Working: A magick ritual.

Yule: Occult holiday, December 22, winter solstice, shortest day of the year.

Occult Symbols

Fig. 1 **The inverted pentagram.**

Fig. 2 **Trail markers. These may be found to show the way to a site.**

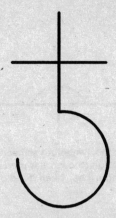

Fig. 3 The Cross of Confusion: This symbol, from the ancient Romans, questions the existence of Jesus Christ and the validity of Christianity.

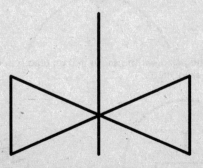

Fig. 4 Anti-Justice: An ancient symbol of justice was the double-bladed axe. Here it is inverted to mean anti-justice.

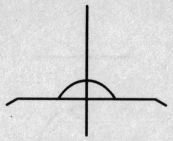

Fig. 5 **Satanic Traitor: This symbolizes someone who has betrayed his Satanic coven. It is used in death threats, rituals of revenge. It has been found on corpses.**

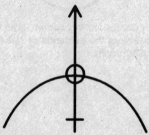

Fig. 6 **Sex magick area: This shows that an area is being used for sexual rituals.**

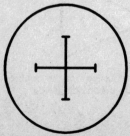

Fig. 8 **Black Mass indicator.**

Fig. 7 **Black Mass indicator.**

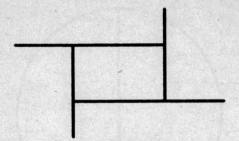

Fig. 9 **Power symbol.**

Fig. 10 **Variations on "666."**

Fig. 11 This symbol meant peace in the 1960's but is being found at occult sites along with a new meaning. It's being called the "Cross of Nero" and means the defeat of Christianity as the cross arms are "broken."

Fig. 12 **No Christianity practiced here.**

N A T A S

N E M A

R E D R U M

Fig. 13 **Satanists are fond of writing words backwards.
Here are several common examples.**

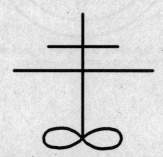

Fig. 14 **This symbol is found in *The Satanic Bible* above the "Nine
Satanic Statements."**

Fig. 15 **This is the sign of the baphomet, a goat head inside an inverted pentagram within two circles.**

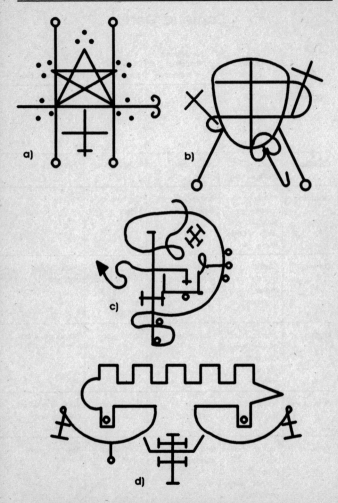

Fig. 16 **These are symbols of lesser demons from ancient beliefs.**
a) Astaroth, b) Baal c) Asmodeus d) Belial.

Santeria Gods

God	Function/ Power	Punishment Inflicted/ Weapons	Christian Syncretization	Necklace Colors
Eleggua	Controls roads, gates, crossroads literally and emotionally	Iron nails	St. Anthony, Christ child	Red and black
Chango	Thunder, fire, lightning	Death, axe, sword	Saint Barbara	Red and white
Obatala	Father of all Saints, source of wisdom and purity	Paralysis, birth defects	Our Lady of Mercy	White
Oshun	Controls gold, money, sex, makes marriages	Abdominal pain, social and domestic strife	Our Lady of La Caridad de Cuba— Patron Saint of Cuba	Yellow, yellow and white
Oggun	Warrior, owns all weapons and metals, controls sorcery	Violent death	Saint Peter	Black and white
Babalu-aye	Patron of sick, skin diseases	Leprosy, gangrene	Saint Lazarus	White and purple or white and light blue
Yemaya	Mother of all Saints, protects women, owns seas, fertility	Respiratory diseases	Our Lady of Regla	Blue and white

Symbols	Appeasement/Sacrifice	Numbers
Cowrie shells, iron rooster	Candy, rum, cigars	3 or any multiple, especially 21
Cups, castles	Lamb, goat, rodent, red rooster	4 and 6
Pearls, white clothing, almost anything white	White bird, female goat	8, 16, 24
Copper, gold, shells, pumpkins	White hen, honey, female goat	5
Agricultural tools, metal necklaces	Blood, feathers, steel knife, railroad tracks	3 and 7
Man on crutches w/dog licking wounds	Cigars, pennies, glasses of water	17
Virgin Mary, usually as a black woman, shells, boats	Duck, turtle, goat, watermelon	7

Santeria Tattoos

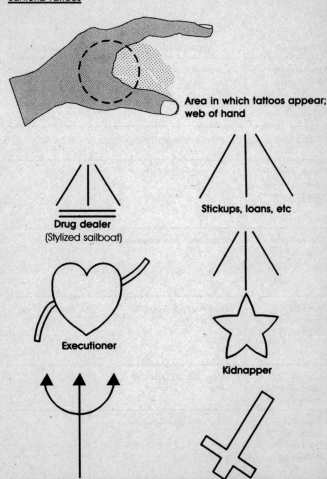

Area in which tattoos appear; web of hand

Drug dealer
(Stylized sailboat)

Stickups, loans, etc

Executioner

Kidnapper

Enforcer

Supplier of Weapons & Equipment

BIBLIOGRAPHY

ADLER, Margot. *Drawing Down the Moon, Witches, Druids, Goddess-Worshippers and Other Pagans in America Today*. Boston: Beacon Press, 1979.

ALHAZRED, Abdul. *Necronomicon*. Edited by Simon. New York: Avon Books, 1977.

AQUINO, Dr. Michael A. *The Crystal Tablet of Set*, 12th Edition. San Francisco, CA: The Temple of Set, 1987.

BISCHOFF, Dr. Erich. *The Kabbala, An Introduction to Jewish Mysticism and Its Secret Doctrine*. York Beach, ME: Samuel Weiser, Inc., 1985 (first published in Germany circa 1910).

CAVENDISH, Richard (editor-in-chief). *Man, Myth and Magic: The Illustrated Encyclopedia of Mythology, Religion and the Unknown*. New York: Marshall Cavendish Corp., 1983.

CAVENDISH, Richard. *The Black Arts*. New York: Perigee Books, 1967.

CROWLEY, Aleister. *The Magical Diaries of Aleister Crowley*. Edited by Stephen Skinner. York Beach, ME: Samuel Weiser, Inc., 1979.

CROWLEY, Aleister. *Magick*. Edited, annotated and introduced by John Symonds and Kenneth Grant. York Beach, ME: Samuel Weiser, Inc., 1974.

DEVINE, M.V. *Brujeria, A Study in Mexican-American Folk-Magic*. St. Paul, MN: Llewellyn Publications, 1982.

HAINING, Peter. *The Anatomy of Witchcraft*. New York: Taplinger Publishing Co., 1972.

HUSON, Paul. *Mastering Witchcraft, A Practical Guide for Witches, Warlocks and Covens*. New York, NY: G.P. Putnam's Sons, 1970.

JONG, Erica. *Witches*. New York: Harry N. Abrams, Inc., Publishers, 1981.

LAVEY, Anton Szandor. *The Satanic Bible*. New York: Avon Books, 1969.

LAVEY, Anton Szandor. *The Satanic Rituals*. New York: Avon Books, 1972.

MAIR, Lucy. *Witchcraft*. New York, Toronto: World University Library, 1969.

MARTELLO, Dr. Leo Louis. *Witchcraft, The Old Religion*. Secaucus: Citadel Press.

MELTON, J. Gordon (editor). *The Encyclopedia of American Religions*. Wilmington, NC: McGrath Publishing Co., 1978 and 1985 supplement.

MICHELET, Jules. *Satanism and Witchcraft, A Study in Medieval Superstition*. New York: The Citadel Press, 1946.

RHODES, H.T.F. *Satanic Mass*. Secaucus, NJ: The Citadel Press, 1974.

ROBBINS, Russell Hope. *The Encyclopedia of Witchcraft and Demonology*. New York: Crown Publishers, Inc., 1969.

SHEINKIN, David, M.D. *Path of the Kabbalah*. New York: Paragon House, Inc., 1986.

SHEPARD, Leslie A. (editor). *Encyclopedia of Occultism and Parapsychology*. Detroit, MI: Gale Research, Co., 1983.

SMITH, Michelle and PAZDER, Lawrence, M.D. *Michelle Remembers*. New York: Congdon and Lattes, Inc., 1980.

VAN DE KAMP, John K. "Report on the Kern County Child Abuse Investigation." Office of the Attorney General, Division of Law Enforcement, Bureau of Investigation, State of California; September 1986.

VERDIER, Paul A., Ph.D. *Brainwashing and the Cults, An Expose on Capturing the Human Mind*. North Hollywood, CA: Wilshire Book Co., 1977.

WIPPLER, Migene Gonzalez. *Rituals and Spells of Santeria*. Bronx, NY: Original Publications, 1984.

WIPPLER, Migene Gonzalez. *The Santeria Experience*. Englewood Cliffs, NJ: Prentice-Hall Inc., 1982.